Digital Finance and Literacy in India

Digital Finance and Literacy in India

Edited by

Abdul Azeez N.P.
Assistant Professor, Department of Economics,
Aligarh Muslim University (AMU), Aligarh

and

S.M. Jawed Akhtar
Professor, Department of Economics,
Aligarh Muslim University (AMU), Aligarh

New Century Publications
New Delhi, India

New Century Publications,
74, Ansari Road, Ground Floor,
Daryaganj, New Delhi – 110 002 (India)

Tel.: 011- 4358 7398, 4101 7798, 2324 7798
E-mail: info@newcenturypublications.com

www.newcenturypublications.com

Editorial office:
4800/24, Ansari Road,
Daryaganj, New Delhi – 110 002

Tel.: 98117 88655

First Published: **2021**

ISBN: **978-81-7708-526-6**

Published by New Century Publications and printed at Milan Enterprises, New Delhi

Designs: Patch Creative Unit, New Delhi

PRINTED IN INDIA

About the Book

Digital finance and literacy have assumed greater significance in 21st century due to complex financial products, prevalence of fraudulent schemes, and deregulation policies of the governments.

In 2020, the world endured an unexpected onslaught by the COVID-19 virus. The shock of the pandemic has been extremely unconventional in terms of its size and uncertainty. The pandemic has been unique in its wide-ranging effects on almost every section of the economy and the society. The virus has posed an unprecedented challenge for policy-making—globally and nationally. It has tested the mettle of policy-makers to deal with uncertain, fluid, complex and dynamic situations, having far-reaching socio-economic implications.

The pandemic and lockdowns have highlighted the importance of digital financial services. Digital financial services enable people to conduct financial transactions remotely using either mobile banking or internet banking. Digital financial transactions do not involve any physical cash exchange and hence prevent the spread of pandemic and helps to keep the economy moving during the pandemic.

Digital financial services are enabling governments to provide quick and secure financial support to *hard-to-reach* people and businesses. This will help mitigate the economic fallout and potentially strengthen the recovery.

Financial literacy enables one to manage one's personal finance in a prudent manner and achieve financial well-being. The objective of any financial literacy programme is to improve knowledge, skills and behaviour of individuals which will lead to awareness and action towards better management of family finances.

This volume contains 11 research papers authored by scholars in the field of digital finance and literacy. Their contributions provide deep insights on various aspects of the subject.

About the Editors

Dr. Abdul Azeez N.P. is currently Assistant Professor, Department of Economics at Aligarh Muslim University (AMU), Aligarh. Prior to joining AMU, he taught at the Department of Economics, Central University of Kashmir, Srinagar, Jammu and Kashmir. He also served as Assistant Professor (Economics) in the Department of Law at AMU, Malappuram Centre, Kerala.

A gold medallist of AMU in M.A. Economics (2010) examination, he obtained Ph.D. degree also from the same University. He also qualified the Junior Research Fellowship (JRF) examination conducted by University Grants Commission (UGC) in 2011. He has published 5 books and numerous research papers in reputed journals. He has participated and presented papers at various national and international conferences. Recently, he has been awarded a major research project on 'Digital and Financial Literacy for Rural India', funded by IMPRESS-ICSSR.

Dr. S.M. Jawed Akhtar is currently Professor, Department of Economics, Aligarh Muslim University (AMU), Aligarh. Presently, he is working as Finance Officer of AMU, Aligarh. He has been actively engaged in teaching and research for more than two decades. He was awarded gold medals for securing first position in B.A. (Hons.) and M.A. (Economics) examinations of the same University.

He has recently completed a major research project on Mahatma Gandhi National Rural Employment Guarantee Scheme (MGNREGS) funded by the UGC. He is also working as Co-Project Director on 'Digital and Financial Literacy for Rural India'. He has authored 12 books and published more than 60 research papers in academically acclaimed journals.

Contents

Contributors

Abdul Azeez N.P.	Assistant Professor, Department of Economics, Faculty of Social Sciences, Aligarh Muslim University, Aligarh.
Bishweshwar Bhattacharjee	Formerly, Research Scholar, Department of Economics, Assam University, Silchar.
Bireshwar Bhattacharjee	Research Scholar, Department of Statistics, Assam University, Silchar.
Elhamuddin Safi	Ph.D. Scholar, Department of Economics, Faculty of Social Sciences, Aligarh Muslim University, Aligarh.
Manasi Gore	Assistant Professor, Savitribai Phule Pune University, Pune.
Mazhar Mohammad	Founder, Chartviewindia.in.
Meenal Annachhatre	Assistant Professor, Savitribai Phule Pune University, Pune.
Mohd. Shafeeq	Research Scholar, Department of Management, Jamia Hamdard, New Delhi.
Nasira Banu M.	Research Scholar, Department of Economics, EMEA College of Arts and Science, Kondotty, Malappuram.
Rajesh Mohapatra	MBA Student, Srusti Academy of Management, Bhubaneswar.
Sana Beg	Assistant Professor, Department of Management, Jamia Hamdard, New Delhi.

Shiva Johri — Associate Professor, Oriental College of Management, Bhopal.

Sumitha Franklin — Assistant Professor, Department of Economics, St. Paul's College, Kalamassery.

V. Sonali — Assistant Professor, Department of MBA, Vignan Institute of Technology and Management (VITAM), Berhampur.

Preface

In 2020, the world endured an unexpected onslaught by the COVID-19 virus. The shock of the pandemic has been extremely unconventional in terms of its size and uncertainty, with its impact dependent on unpredictable factors like intensity of lockdowns, extent of supply chain and financial market disruptions alongside societal response to the associated public health measures. The pandemic has been unique in its wide-ranging effects on almost every section of the economy and the society. The virus has posed an unprecedented challenge for policy-making, globally and nationally. It has tested the mettle of policy-makers to deal with uncertain, fluid, complex and dynamic situations having far-reaching socio-economic implications. It has also tested the frontiers of medical science, which rose to the challenge by developing an effective vaccine within a year.

The pandemic has threatened all that was taken for granted, viz. mobility, safety, and a normal life itself. This, in turn, posed the most formidable economic challenge to India and to the world. The pandemic and the lockdowns have highlighted the importance of digital financial services. Digital financial services enable people to conduct financial transactions remotely using either mobile banking or internet banking. Digital financial transactions do not involve any physical cash exchange and hence prevent the spread of pandemic and helps to keep the economy moving during the pandemic.

According to International Monetary Fund (IMF), during the COVID-19 lockdown, digital financial services are enabling governments to provide quick and secure financial support to *hard-to-reach* people and businesses. This will help mitigate the economic fallout and potentially strengthen the recovery. Also, to tap the high potential of digital financial services in the post-COVID era, many factors need to fall into place.

Financial literacy has assumed greater significance in 21st century due to complex financial products, prevalence of fraudulent schemes, deregulation policies of regulators and government. Financial literacy enables one to manage one's personal finance in a prudent manner and achieve financial wellbeing. The objective of any financial literacy programme is to improve knowledge, skills and behaviour of individuals which will lead to awareness and action towards better management of their and family finances.

Financial literacy is the possession of a set of skills and knowledge which allow an individual to make informed and effective decisions with all of his financial resources. Understanding basic financial concepts allows people to know how to navigate in the financial system.

Lack of awareness of digital financial literacy, especially among the rural population is a major challenge in the country, more so in light of the plans to make India a cashless economy. There is an urgent need to create awareness among the citizens, especially in rural and semi-urban areas regarding digital finance services and also enable/support in access to digital finance services options.

We place on record our deep sense of gratitude to all the scholars who have contributed to this volume. Their scholarly papers would surely add to the existing body of literature on the subject. We also thank the editorial and production teams of New Century Publications, New Delhi for the cooperation and help to publish this book in an elegant manner.

Aligarh

Abdul Azeez N.P.
S.M. Jawed Akhtar

1

Digital Financial Services during COVID-19 Lockdown in India

Nasira Banu M.

Introduction

The coronavirus (COVID-19) pandemic has disrupted the economic activities all over the world. India has been no exception to this. The Government of India, in March 2020, imposed the most stringent lockdown in the world to contain the spread of the pandemic. However, the economic crisis due to lockdown eventually led to the un-lockdown phase in India after June 2020 even though the pandemic still prevailed. The pandemic and the lockdown have highlighted the importance of financial inclusion and mainly, digital financial inclusion. The Rangarajan Committee Report defined financial inclusion as, 'the process of ensuring access to financial services and timely and adequate credit where needed by vulnerable groups such as weaker sections and low-income groups at an affordable cost'. Digital financial inclusion is defined by CGAP as 'digital access to and use of formal financial services by excluded and underserved populations. Such services should be suited to customers' needs, and delivered responsibly, at a cost both affordable to customers and sustainable for providers'.

Digital financial services enable people to conduct financial transactions remotely using either mobile banking or internet banking. Digital financial services provide easy access to financial services which is very low in India. [1] Digital financial transactions do not involve any physical cash exchange and hence prevent the spread of pandemic and helps to keep the economy moving during the pandemic. According to International Monetary Fund (IMF), during the COVID-19 lockdown, digital financial services enabled governments to provide quick and secure financial support to "hard-to-reach" people and businesses, as demonstrated in Namibia, Peru, Zambia, and Uganda. This helped mitigate the economic fallout and potentially strengthened the recovery.

Also, to tap the high potential of digital financial services in the post-COVID era, many factors need to fall in place. Equal access to digital infrastructure (access to electricity, mobile and internet coverage, and digital ID); greater financial and digital literacy; and the avoidance of data biases are necessary for a more inclusive recovery.

With the introduction of Digital India initiative in 2015, there has been a paradigm shift towards the digitalization of financial services. As per India's National Strategy for Financial Inclusion (2019-24), digital financial services will be strengthened in all the tier II and tier VI centres by 2022, to achieve a cashless society. The Committee has recommended that every village should have a financial service provider within a radius of 5 km. to enable universal access to financial services. After the Digital India initiative, two events majorly contributed to the digitalization of the Indian economy. The first one was the demonetization of ₹ 500 and ₹ 1000 currency notes in 2016 by the government, aimed at curtailing the shadow economy in India and achieving a cashless economy.

Another event was the outbreak of COVID-19 pandemic which led to exchange of cash being unsafe, thus prompting the use of digital transactions. The present paper analyses the use of digital payment systems before and during the lockdown to evaluate India's preparedness in achieving the objective of digital financial inclusion and provide important policy implications.

The Background

While a lot of literature is available on financial inclusion, literature on digital financial inclusion (DFI) and digital financial services (DFS) has come to the forefront recently. In this context, some of the studies on financial inclusion, DFI and DFS, have been reviewed to find out the gaps in available literature and the present paper.

There have been numerous studies which have highlighted the importance of financial inclusion and digital financial inclusion. Financial deepening accelerates economic growth by making finance available to those lacking adequate finance. Financial depth of India is much lower than that of the Asian countries. Two major factors identified as a consequence of financial exclusion are: (i) complications in day-to-day cash flow management, and (ii) lack of financial planning and security due to absence of access to bank accounts.

The impact of financial development on economic growth is most pronounced at the lower income levels. Poor developing countries will gain the most from the growth and development of the financial sector. Also, the link between financial development and income inequality has been found to be quadratic, implying that at a low level of development, financial development is likely to be positively related to inequality, but once a threshold level of development is achieved, the link between the two becomes negative.

Digital financial inclusion has also gained significant importance in recent times, especially, among the emerging and developed economies. A positive relationship between digital finance and financial inclusion is stronger for high- and middle-income users while the relationship may be non-linear or negative for poor users of digital finance who refuse to use such services due to reasons like superstitions, unaffordable fees, financial illiteracy and many others. The article has found two-way causality between digital finance and financial inclusion.

There is a significant positive relationship of financial literacy and digital financial usage with financial inclusion. Internet usage plays a mediating role between financial literacy and financial inclusion and had an indirect effect on financial inclusion through digital financial product usage. Reducing the cost and improving financial literacy of residents to popularize internet usage can promote the use of digital financial products and achieve the goal of advancing financial inclusion. Digital financial literacy is also a significant contributor to digital financial inclusion and the relationship between them has been found to be really strong.

Another finding suggests that financial knowledge and risk tolerance are significantly and positive correlated with the likelihood to use digital financial services. Also, the likelihood of using digital financial service increases with the respondent being male and having a university degree. Age was found to be negatively and significantly correlated with using digital financial services (Königsheim et al., 2017).

A huge gap of 20 percentage points was found between current use and future potential usage with regard to fintech as well as digital finance solutions. Performance efficiency, economic benefit, convenience, security risk, technical conditions and habit, positively affect the future usage intention while hedonic motivation has a negative effect. Economic benefit was rated the highest for digital finance solutions (Gerlach and Lutz, 2019).

Digital financial inclusion has reduced people's ability to insure themselves against transitory income shocks which is due to the fact that consumption becomes oversensitive to income with the online purchase of food. Also, contrary to DFI, traditional financial sector development contributes to better household consumption smoothing against transitory income shocks (Lai et al., 2020).

After reviewing the available literature, it is evident that there is a lot of literature available on the importance, determinants of financial inclusion and DFI and the issues associated with them. However, there are very few studies related to the impact of lockdown on DFS in India. The paper, therefore, analyses the impact of the India's most stringent lockdown in the world on different type of digital payments. The analysis will reveal if a country like India is prepared for digital financial inclusion (DFI) whereas per Global Findex Data, 2017,190 million adults in India are still unbanked. The paper will help in policy-making decisions for expanding the use of digital financial services by targeting issues identified in the use of digital financial services during the lockdown.

Objectives of the Study

The lockdown has highlighted the important role of digital financial services in the smooth functioning of an economy. With the restrictions imposed on the movement of people due to the lockdown, digital financial services provided an easy way to make money transfers to family, acquaintances and also to carry out various financial transactions, using the digital mode. However, appropriate availability of digital infrastructure, digital literacy, data security and various other factors are also important to facilitate DFS. 92 percent of the Indian workforce exists in the informal sector and mainly depends on the cash mode for transactions. This makes it difficult for them to use DFS. Since DFI is a way forward to financial inclusion, people need to be financially included first to enhance the use of DFS.

However, despite numerous initiatives by the Government of India, many people and the regions still remain unbanked and under-banked which is a hurdle in the pathway to DFS. Therefore, the use of digital payment services during the lockdown can provide an important insight into India's economic environment conduciveness for the use of DFS. In accordance with the above discussion, the objectives of the paper are as follows:

1. To analyse digital payment services before and during the lockdown to evaluate India's preparedness to achieve digital financial inclusion.
2. To identify issues in India's path towards digital financial inclusion.

Methodology

The paper is based on the secondary data. The secondary data on 7 digital payment transactions has been evaluated in the present paper. The data on immediate payment service (IMPS), united payment interface (UPI), unstructured supplementary service data (USSD) service (*99#) and Aadhaar-enabled payment system (AEPS) transactions was obtained from the National Payments Corporation of India (NPCI) database while the data on mobile banking, real time gross settlement (RTGS) and national electronic funds transfer (NEFT) transactions was obtained from the RBI database to provide authenticity to the data.

The paper considers the monthly data for the period September 2019 to June 2020, for all the 7 transaction modes for a better analysis. To incorporate the impact of lockdown, the paper undertakes analysis of the digital payment transactions for the two periods, viz., before the lockdown period and during the lockdown period. The data from September 2019 to February 2020 represents the trends of digital payments before the lockdown and the data from March 2020 to June 2020 presents trends for the period of lockdown. The data has been analysed using statistical tools such as percentages and growth rates. Data from several reports was also used to meet the objectives of the study. The paper is mainly descriptive and analytical in nature.

Various Digital Financial Services (DFS)

The DFI efficiency is best measured by the growth rates in digital payment transactions. In order to analyse the impact of lockdown on digital financial services, the paper takes into account data regards 7 digital payment transactions, namely, IMPS, UPI, USSD service (*99#), AEPS, mobile banking, RTGS and NEFT. Though the analysis involves the data on mobile banking, data on USSD service has also been undertaken to specially focus on the impact of pandemic on people who do not have network connectivity and rely on mobile SMS based services for financial transactions. The analysis is hypothesised on the assumption that lockdown during pandemic displayed increased positive growth rates in digital transactions.

IMPS: IMPS transactions, introduced in 2010, are used to make inter-bank electronic transfer of funds. The service allows transfer of funds at any point of time including during bank holidays, i.e., it is a 24x7x365 facility.

It was observed that while there were fluctuations in the IMPS transactions before the lockdown also but there was a significant fall in the growth rate of both IMPS volume and amount of transactions from March 2020 onwards with the a very steep fall in April 2020 when the lockdown was at its peak. While the lockdown was announced towards the end of March 2020, the pandemic entered India in the month of February 2020 itself which explains the significant fall in IMPS transactions after February 2020.

In May 2020, the government allowed certain relaxations in regions where COVID-19 had been contained which justifies a significant increase in the growth rate of both volume and amount of IMPS transactions. After increasing in the month of May 2020, growth rate for both the transactions again witnessed a decline in June 2020 due to the bleak outlook for the Indian economy. The analysis depicts a significant negative impact of the lockdown on IMPS transactions.

United Payment Interface (UPI): UPI is an instant retail payment system which facilitates inter-bank transactions. Unlike IMPS, most banks do not charge fee on UPI transactions which is simpler and secure to carry out.

It was observed that the lockdown resulted in negative growth rate in both the volumes and amounts of UPI transactions. UPI transaction growth rates followed the same trend as did the IMPS transactions, i.e., they plummeted in April 2020, surged in the May 2020 due to the relaxations and then again slumped in the month of June 2020.This signifies that the negative impact of lockdown on UPI transactions was significant.

AEPS: AEPS allows every person to conduct financial transactions through Aadhar-based identification. Customers having bank accounts linked to Aadhar have to provide their Aadhar verification at point of sale (POS), to carry out transactions like funds transfer, cash deposit, cash withdrawal, etc. [2] A different picture of the growth rate of AEPS approved transactions, in comparison to IMPS, UPI and USSD service transactions was noticed. While the AEPS transactions witnessed negative growth rates in February 2020 and March 2020, there was a significant positive growth rate in April 2020 in contrast to the above transactions.

The positive growth rate during the most stringent lockdown is explained by the fact that the Government of India announced a relief package of ₹ 1.7 lakh crore under the Pradhan Mantri Garib Kalyan Yojana during the lockdown. The government made cash transfers to those who were most affected by the lockdown which justifies the positive growth rate of AEPS approved transactions in April 2020. However, AEPS approved transactions again saw a negative growth rate in May 2020 and June 2020. Thus, the impact of lockdown on AEPS transaction was positive rather than negative.

Mobile Banking: Mobile banking enables people to carry out financial transactions remotely using their mobile phones. Mobile banking can be provided by financial institutions either through SMS, USSD or mobile phone applications. Mobile banking has the potential to reach the unbanked and under-banked regions due to high level of active mobile users in the country.

During the lockdown, both the volume and amount of mobile banking transactions registered a negative growth rate. The negative growth rate in mobile banking transactions continued till April 2020, similar to the above transactions while witnessing positive growth rate in May 2020 when the relaxations were announced by the Government of India.

However, the growth rate slumped again in June 2020 due to apprehensions about the future of economy. Hence, mobile banking transactions also displayed a similar negative impact of the lockdown as regards the use of digital financial services.

RTGS Payments: RTGS payments are used to make instantaneous inter-fund transfers. The term 'real time' means that the payments are processed immediately as they are received and 'gross settlement' means that the individual funds transfer is settled individually.

It was revealed that positive growth rates in the volume of RTGS transactions turned into negative immediately after the lockdown started. However, the growth rate of volume grew significantly in May 2020 due to the relaxations announced, although falling again in June 2020 but yet remaining positive. On the other hand, while the amount of RTGS transactions was already fluctuating between positive and negative growth rates before the lockdown, the growth rate was significantly negative in April 2020 when the lockdown was at its peak and positive after May 2020 due to the similar reasons. The analysis revealed a negative impact of the lockdown on RTGS transactions albeit for a lesser period of time.

NEFT Payments: NEFT payments system, initiated in 2015, is a one-to-one funds transfer. Funds can be transferred only between two NEFT-enabled bank accounts. However, unlike RTGS, funds transfer through NEFT is settled in pre-defined hourly batches.

The analysis of NEFT transactions showed a fluctuating trend, both in terms of the volume and amount throughout the period of study. However, the negative growth in April 2020 was very low, revealing the effect of lockdown. The growth rate again turned positive from May 2020 onwards.

***99#, USSD Service:** *99# is a USSD service which takes banking services to the reach of every common man through mobile banking. The use of this service does not require a connection to the internet, benefiting people and regions without network connectivity. Various services can be availed by the customer, just by dialling *99# on their mobile phones. The number is common for all the telecom service providers (TSPs). The analysis showed that the transactions, in terms of both numbers and amount, slumped in February 2020. The growth rates, after declining in February 2020, remained zero for the volume of transactions from March 2020 onwards till May 2020, while the amount of transactions continuously witnessed a negative growth rate until April 2020. The positive growth rate in the volume of *99# transactions was witnessed only in June 2020.

The above analysis implies that the lockdown had a negative impact on mobile banking transactions also. However, the effect of the pandemic and lockdown on the volume and amount of USSD transactions was low in comparison to other transactions which reflect the potential of USS services to accomplish the agenda of digital financial inclusion in India.

Even though there was evidence of significant negative growth rates during the lockdown period with respect to all the digital transactions except AEPS and low impact on USSD service, there was a trend of positive growth rates from May 2020 onwards, reflecting the future potential of DFS following the unlocking phase.

Identifying Issues in Digital Financial Inclusion (DFI)

The above analysis leads us to identify the challenges that the Indian economy is facing in its journey towards DFI. India has undertaken many initiatives to increase the level of financial inclusion and digital financial inclusion including the Pradhan Mantri Jan Dhan Yojana (PMJDY), electronic benefit transfers, easing the KYC requirements and many other initiatives to eliminate price and non-price barriers. However, there are still certain issues in India's DFI which need to be addressed.

Despite all the initiatives, many accounts remain inactive. In India, the share of inactive accounts is a staggering 48 percent—highest in the world and about twice the average of 25 percent for developing economies (Demirguc-Kunt et al., 2018).

The primary for this reason is the lack of appropriate financial products which are best suited to the needs of different sections of the society. The specific needs of various sections of the society for different kinds of financial products needs to be recognised to design suitable financial products for all. This will facilitate financial inclusion and further adoption of DFS also as financial inclusion is a prerequisite for DFI.

Since the lockdown resulted in negative growth rates of digital payment transactions, it implies that India is still a cash dominant economy to a larger extent. [3] There is a lack of trust among people in digital payment systems, mainly among those people who are not so much technology friendly. Even though the cash transfers made by the government to the poor people led to a sudden surge in growth rates of AEPS transactions, yet the growth rates surged back significantly to the previous levels in May 2020.

The consumer protection risks associated with digital transactions explains this to a larger extent. The risks faced by low-income people who are the recipients of cash transfers—whether government to person (G2P) or donor to person (D2P)—directly in their bank accounts include: (i) inability to transact due to network or service unreliability; (ii) insufficient agents or automatic teller machines (ATMs); (iii) complex user interfaces and payment processes; (iv) poor or no recourse mechanism; and (v) fraud that targets recipients (Zimmerman and Yezback, 2020).

An appropriate digital infrastructure is key to achieving DFI successfully. However, lack of internet connectivity and inadequate digital financial infrastructure still prevails in many regions, preventing people to access DFS. The fact that lack of digital financial infrastructure leads to low level of digital financial services has also been proved empirically (Naumenkova et al., 2020).

Another challenge for DFI is the lack of financial and digital literacy among many people, mainly among low-income people, females, less educated and the rural people. People are not aware of the benefits associated with the use of DFS and even about the various financial services available through digital modes. There is a tendency among people to still rely on traditional bank branches to carry out the financial transactions as they are still not comfortable using the technology-based platforms.

Digital divide is also prevalent in the Indian economy to a large extent which has become a hurdle in the use of DFS. As per the global Findex Data, 2017, men are twice as likely as women to have access to both the mobile phones and the internet in some economies, including Bangladesh, Ethiopia, and India. Ramping up digital financial services with pre-existing divides in the use of digital financial services, risks exacerbating inequalities (Agur et al., 2020).

Access to finance is one the foremost factors required to facilitate DFS. Digital finance should improve the welfare of individuals and businesses that have formal bank accounts and have funds in their bank accounts to complete multiple financial transactions (Ozili, 2018). The loss of livelihoods and hence the income due to the lockdown, explains the negative growth rates in various digital transactions.

Hence, just developing the infrastructure and providing financial and digital literacy will not suffice to achieve the objective of DFI. There is a need to ensure that no one lives in poverty and sufficient cash transfers are made to the poor people to prevent any disruption in the functioning of DFS. There is a need to ensure that people are provided with a secure employment to avoid such disruptions during any crisis.

Conclusions and Policy Implications

Digital financial services provide a convenient and easy way to carry out financial transactions. COVID-19 pandemic and the resultant lockdown to contain its spread has highlighted the importance of digital financial services even more in the recent times. The present paper used secondary data pertaining to seven digital payment options to analyse digital financial transactions namely, IMPS, UPI, USSD service, AEPS, mobile banking, RTGS and NEFT. The paper hypothesised on the premise that the lockdown would have resulted in positive growth rates of various digital transactions.

The results, however, came contrary to the premise. The lockdown resulted in negative growth rates with respect to various digital transactions, implying that despite so many initiatives by the Government of India, the country is still not fully prepared to achieve its objective of complete digital financial inclusion.

It was just the AEPS transactions which witnessed a positive growth rate when the lockdown was its peak which highlights the need to design suitable financial products and services according to the needs of different sections of the society, particularly the low-income people and other vulnerable groups.

The analysis provides some important policy implications for digital financial inclusion. Government of India needs to augment the required digital financial infrastructure to facilitate smooth functioning of DFS.

Government should organise digital and financial awareness programmes, specifically targeting the needs of people who still remain financially or digitally excluded. The current programmes by the government to spread financially literacy also needs to be administered well.

Another important policy implication is that before ramping up the use of digital financial services, the issue of digital divide should be addressed to prevent exacerbation of already existing inequalities.

People in the informal economy should be provided with secure employment to avoid any disruptions in the cash flow during the crisis. Consumer protection rules in digital transactions also need to be framed well so that people develop trust in carrying out digital financial transactions.

Endnotes

1. According to Financial Access Survey data by International Monetary Fund (IMF), number of automatic teller machines (ATMs) per 1,00,000 adults was just 20.95 and number of commercial bank branches per 1,00,000 adults was just 14.58 in 2019.
2. AEPS transactions include ONUS transactions as well as OFFUS transactions.
3. As per the RBI data, currency with public increased from ₹ 20,52,209 crore on March 31, 2020 to ₹ 21,16,677 crore on June 21, 2020.

References

Agur, I., Peria, S.M. and Rochon, C. (2020), "Digital Financial Services and the Pandemic: Opportunities and Risks for Emerging and Developing Economies", 1-13.

Demirguc-Kunt, A., Klapper, L., Singer, D., Ansar, S. and Hess, J. (2018), "The Global Findex Database 2017: Measuring Financial Inclusion and the Fintech Revolution", Washington D.C.: World Bank, available at: https://doi.org/10.1596/978-1-4648-1259-0.

Eriksson von Allmen, U., Khera, P., Ogawa, S. and Ratna, S. (2020), "Digital Financial Inclusion in the Times of COVID-19", IMF, July, 1-7, available at: https://blogs.imf.org/2020/07/01/digital-financial-inclusion-in-the-times-of-covid-19.

Gerlach, J.M. and Lutz, J.K.T. (2019), "Evidence on Usage Behavior and Future Adoption Intention of Fintechs and Digital Finance Solutions", *The International Journal of Business and Finance Research*, 13(2), 83-105.

Jalilian, H. and Kirkpatrick, C. (2005), "Does Financial Development Contribute to Poverty Reduction?", *Journal of Development Studies*, 41(4), 636-656, available at: https://doi.org/10.1080/00220380500092754.

Königsheim, C., Lukas, M. And Nöth, M. (2017), "Financial Knowledge, Risk Preferences, and the Demand for Digital Financial Services", *Schmalenbach Business Review*, 18(4), 343-375, available at:

https://doi.org/10.1007/s41464-017-0040-0.

Lai, J.T., Yan, I.K. M., Yi, X. and Zhang, H. (2020), "Digital Financial Inclusion and Consumption Smoothing in China", 28(1), 64-93, available at: https://doi.org/10.1111/cwe.12312.

Layman, T. and Lauer, K. (2015), "What is Digital Financial Inclusion and Why Does it Matter?", March, 1-5, available at: https://librarynews.lmu.edu/2018/03/what-is-digital-pedagogy-and-why-does-it-matter.

Mohan, R. (2006), "Economic Growth, Financial Deepening and Financial Inclusion", *Reserve Bank of India Bulletin*, November 2, 1-18, available at: http://www.rakeshmohan.com/docs/RBIBulletinNov2006-2.pdf.

Naumenkova, S., Mishchenko, S. and Dorofeiev, D. (2020), "Digital Financial Inclusion: Evidence from Ukraine", available at: https://doi.org/10.21511/imfi.16(3).2019.18.

Ozili, P.K. (2018), "Impact of Digital Finance on Financial Inclusion and Stability", *Borsa Istanbul Review*, 18(4), 329-340, available at: https://doi.org/10.1016/j.bir.2017.12.003.

RBI (2008), "Financial Inclusion", Mumbai: Reserve Bank of India, available at: https://www.rbi.org.in/scripts/PublicationsView.aspx?id=10494.

RBI (2012), "National Strategy for Financial Inclusion", June.

Shen, Y., Hu, W. and Hueng, C.J. (2018), "The Effects of Financial Literacy, Digital Financial Product Usage and Internet Usage on Financial Inclusion in China", MATEC Web of Conferences, 228, available at: https://doi.org/10.1051/matecconf/201822805012.

Tony, N. and Desai, K. (2020), "Impact of Digital Financial Literacy on Digital Financial Inclusion", *International Journal of Scientific and Technology Research*, 9(1), 1911-1915.

2

Digital Sale of Farm Produce

Meenal Annachhatre

Introduction

Despite the complexities, agitations and diversities, Indian farmers have a remarkable success story. Agriculture production continues to grow and export markets are offering huge opportunities for farmers. Agriculture is one of the few bright spots in an economy ravaged by COVID-19. Agriculture as a sector, works as a residual sponge in India. People just migrate out of farming, mostly voluntarily, in search of better paying employment. Farming always works as a backup plan for them.

According to the CMIE data, 111.3 million people declared their occupation as farming in 2019-20. By March 2020, this had increased to 117 million and shooting further to 130 million in June 2020. An exceptional performance of agriculture during the pandemic is well supported by the Reserve Bank of India (RBI) data. In other words, the sector added ₹ 14,815 crore in the first three months of the fiscal 2019-2020 in absolute monetary terms. This comes as a silver lining in the entire pandemic situation. Alongside agriculture, telecom and digital services have kept India moving despite fears and lockdowns around the virus. Now, the challenge ahead, with the introduction of Farm Bills in 2020, is to marry small and medium farmers with digital techniques and services. This is mainly for empowering small and medium farmers with digital techniques to utilize the proposed market structure.

If we just brief the history of large agricultural reforms in India, we will notice that all of the reforms were either farm-centric or production-centric and never paid attention to the income gains for farmers. Like any other economic activity or business, farmers do work for profits and income. With Farm Bills 2020, the Government of India is trying to sell the new market-centric and farmer's income related reforms for the first time.

Ashok Dalwai, an agricultural economist; additional secretary, Ministry of Agriculture and Farmers' Welfare; and CEO of the National Rainfed Area Authority, opined that after Green Revolution and White Revolution, India needs to move towards the 'Income Revolution'. If we are really taking this big step of market-centric reforms and well coined term like 'income revolution', we have to have a well-established network of digital technology and services to access the market. Not only do we need efficiencies in productivity and reduced costs of production, but we also need effective monetization of farm produce. With this transformation, we expect the digital innovation to enable these critical shifts. The entire value chain, right from fields up to the stage where the farmers are able to realize money in their pockets, smart use of information and communication technology (ICT) would strengthen farmers' position.

This paper has exclusively focused on the National Commodity and Derivatives Exchange (NCDEX) and the Farmer Producers Organizations (FPOs) functioning in enabling the marginalized farmers to acquire skills for online trading, getting into future contracts, understanding the underlying risks and settling those contracts with good accessibility and knowledge of digital finance.

The Farm Acts, 2020

In the wake of COVID-19, Government of India promulgated three Ordinances on June 5, 2020 relating to agriculture, which were subsequently replaced by the Acts of Parliament.

The Farmers (Empowerment and Protection) Agreement on Price Assurance and Farm Services Act, 2020, is a dedicated legislation to enable contract farming based on written agreements. The intent is to make sure that investment flows into the agricultural sector.

The Farmers' Produce Trade and Commerce (Promotion and Facilitation) Act, 2020, liberates farmers by giving them the freedom to sell anywhere. It is expected to facilitate lucrative prices for farmers through competitive alternative trading channels to promote barrier-free intra-state and inter-state trade of agricultural goods. The Act also permits electronic trading of farmers' produce in the specified trade areas.

The Essential Commodities (Amendment) Act, 2020 has the objective of restricting the conditions on which the government can impose stock limit on agricultural produce.

Main intention is to help small and marginal farmers (86 percent of total farmers) who do not have either means to bargain for their produce to get a better price and grow further. The provision in the bill on agriculture market allows farmers to sell their produce outside the APMC *mandis* to whomsoever they want. Here, farmers are surely going to get a better price through competition. This provision will also help farmers to save on the transportation cost. Removal of cereals, pulses, onions, potatoes, oilseeds and edible oil from the list of essential commodities as per the legislation will do away with the stock holding limits on these items.

The legislation on contract farming will allow farmers to get into contract with agri-buisness firms or big retailers on pre-agreed prices for their produce. It would facilitate lucrative prices for the farmers via alternative trading channels to promote barrier-free intra-state and inter-state trade of agriculture produce. Along with various provisions, the Bills allow electronic trading of scheduled farmers' produce (agricultural produce regulated under any state APMC Act) in the specified trade area. It will also facilitate direct and online buying and selling of the agricultural produce, i.e. in futures market via electronic devices and internet. At this point, the question of efficient and effective use of digital technology and digital finances by farmers assumes critical importance.

Here, we need to refer to The Forward Contracts (Regulation) Amendment Bill, 2010 which was introduced by the Minister of Agriculture, Consumer Affairs, Food and Public Distribution. Main intention was to give farmers a free hand to sell their produce in the futures market at a predetermined price. While the commodity futures market has grown by 40 percent annually in the past few years, most of the growth has taken place in non-agricultural commodities, and farmers have for various reasons kept away from the futures market and did not hedge their produce against price risk. Of the many reasons, one major reason of not indulging themselves in the commodity futures market is little awareness among small and marginal farmers about digital finance and digital techniques of trading.

Going by the advocates of the new Farm Bills, 2020, we can very well state that the new bills are about empowering small and marginal farmers who were always exposed to the market unpredictability and price uncertainties. Giving them the options of alternative trading channels like futures and options market trading facilities will help them in improving their realisation, which they generally lose to middlemen.

Digital Services and Farmers

Financial services are essential for an economy. While undertaking any business or economic activity, or even for household needs, financial services are required to spend, save, invest and protect against risks. Any producer who would wish to hedge [1] his/her produce against the risk of unpredictable price movements or market fluctuations, would use hedging instruments like futures and options market contracts. And farmers are no exception to it. These hedging instruments are very much a part of financial services, or to be very precise, of digital financial services because futures and option contracts are traded on exchange. This very nature of hedging tools calls for participants to be well versed with digital techniques of trading and digital financial services.

In case of small and medium farmers, utilization of future trading contract, encompass two main issues. Firstly, on any future trading exchange—be it currency or commodity—size of the contract, i.e. quantity or volume is standardized. Usually, small and medium farmers do not reach up to that standard size of the contract and are unable to make use of these online future trading facilities. Secondly, they are not well equipped with the digital techniques and do not know how to go for the settlement of these digital finances.

Preamble to the 2013 National Policy for Promotion of Farmer Producer Organizations (FPOs) says, "collectivization of producers, especially small and marginal farmers, into producer organizations has emerged as one of the most effective pathways to address the many challenges of agriculture but most importantly, improved access to investments, technology and inputs and markets".

FPOs have to deal with varied business activities related to the farm produce and work for the benefit of the member producers through economies of scale which is the solution to most of the challenges faced by small farmers. In the Union Budget for 2019-20, the Union Finance Minister set a target of creating 10,000 FPOs in the next five years. The National Commodity & Derivatives Exchange (NCDEX), established in year 2003, is primarily dealing in agricultural commodities in India. NCDEX has also been given the responsibility of intensifying FPOs activities and improve farmers' participation in the agri-future trade at NCDEX. However, analysis by Tirtha Chatterji, Raghav Raghunathan and Ashok Gulati in August 2019, highlighted that between April 2016 and May 2018, only a tiny fraction (0.004 percent) of overall agri-futures trade at NCDEX was through FPOs.

NCDEX, in line with government's vision of doubling farmers' income, has introduced several initiatives to provide farmers with access to commodity derivatives market to mitigate their price risks. Further, NCDEX has been handholding FPOs through a number of initiatives such as price dissemination through free SMS service, awareness cum training programmes across the country, reaching out to farmers through dedicated TV show viz. "mandi.com" on DD Kisan, among others. These initiatives have been able to encourage more and more FPOs to use commodity derivatives platform as a transparent and fair alternate market platform thereby ensuring that they are able to manage their price risk. [2]

Ashok Gulati's paper, titled, 'Linking Farmers to Futures Market in India', puts forward few important suggestions for FPOs, NCDEX and also for the Government for better participation of small and medium farmers in the agri-future trading. One suggestion, not very explicitly mentioned in the paper, is about the handholding and upgrading of knowledge and awareness of small and medium scale farmers regarding futures trading and helping farmers to secure their business against price fluctuations and market uncertainties.

For this kind of handholding and capacity building of small farmers, digital techniques and digital finance is a necessary prerequisite. Digital finance encompasses provisions, wherein individuals and companies can have access to payments, savings, and credit products without even stepping into a bank branch. This is possible through digitization, which can essentially turn a smart phone into a wallet, a cheque book, a bank branch, and an accounting ledger—all in one. Digital technology innovations have huge potentials to drive positive impacts for small-scale producers. It can come in any forms like input supply, finances, insurance, farm management, market access, linkages, etc. With reference to improving small and marginal farmers' participation in the agri-future and also in the commodity option trading to hedge their price risk, India needs to build up and augment digital infrastructure and digital financial facilities at farmers' doorstep.

Access to internet, appropriate electronic devices to check exchange movements and farmers taking their positions accordingly in the futures market, is what we are looking for. Providing these tools and other infrastructure to each and every farmer in each and every district and taluka is challenging for a big country like India. Here, the role of Farm Produce Organizations (FPOs) is very crucial, not only as facilitators but also by linking farmers with futures and derivatives market. Evidently, the Ministry of Agriculture and Farmers Welfare along with NCDEX can spread the network of FPOs and empowering their capacities in the remotest part of the country which will enable small and medium farmers in many ways. This will also lead to financial inclusion and that too of digital type.

Option contract also works the way in which future exchange works. Option contracts also have a standard size of contract and are traded on the exchange. In case of option contracts, as a hedging tool, trader has to pay the premium upfront and would sell the produce in the futures market at a pre-determined price and on a pre-specified date. On the day of contract expiry, if the spot price in the market has moved in favour of the farmer due to some reasons, the farmer can cancel his option contract on the exchange by just forgoing the upfront premium paid, and then avail the higher price in the spot market and earn profits.

For all this to function smoothly, an established network of information and communication technology is mandatory and to settle those contracts, as per the price movements in the market, farmers' need 'digital finance'.

Remarks and Conclusions

Commodity exchanges [3] have proven to be effective institutional mechanisms for enhancing the efficiency and competitiveness of agricultural markets in many emerging economies. Use of commodity exchanges by Chinese farmers needs to be cited here since China has almost 80 percent of small and marginal farmers representing their agriculture sector. Those 80 percent Chinese small and medium farmers have proved their competitiveness in the international market through their exports.

Evidence suggests that structured trade through contract-based commodity exchanges may provide several benefits which are not present in physical commodity markets. For example, price discovery (market prices based on underlying supply/demand, minimizing the possibility of intermediaries capturing large portions of the final market price without adding much value, market transparency (access to information on the number of buyers and sellers and quantities available on the market), and price risk management (protection against commodity price variation). Additionally, commodity exchanges may reduce many key transaction costs (such as costs involved in identifying a buyer or seller), improving access to finance, and protecting buyers and sellers from broken or inadequately fulfilled contracts.

For all this, the basic requirement along with good governance, regulatory body, and macroeconomic stability, is the availability of digital techniques to get into the contracts on the exchange and digital finance to clear and settle the contract as a part of clearing and settlement services. Each country's commodity exchange markets would vary in their potential in numerable ways. However, a wide body of literature has indicated that where the commodity exchanges are effectively designed, they can deliver a variety of benefits to commodity market participants.

As stated earlier, Indian agriculture is currently at crossroads, not only because of the introduction of New Farm Bill, 2020, but also because now we have our market-led crop insurance scheme with digital innovations. This is so because we are using geo-tagging, satellite data, and drone technology to verify crop-cutting experiments. To build the land data, we have started using geo-tagging and geo-imagery. This also enables in settlement of crop insurance claims in a faster and easier way. Currently, the disputes are being settled by using satellite images and drone technology. If this is the junction of an interesting crossroad in Indian Agriculture, then we also have to add this new pathway for a more effective and efficient utilization of agricultural commodity exchanges with the help of digital techniques and digital finance.

Commodity exchange boards would help the farmers discover a better price for their produce in India. We are emphasizing the price aspect of the commodity exchanges because Indian farmers have been dependent on minimum support prices (MSPs) for so many years. If any further agricultural reforms in India have to happen, they have to happen now. It is high time to make our farmers competitive enough to fetch a considerable market share with real good returns.

Arriving at a price that accurately reflects underlying supply and demand (in other words, price discovery) occurs on an exchange with sufficient volume and number of transactions relative to the overall trade in the physical market. When trade on an exchange represents only a small fraction of overall trade in the market, the prices of goods traded on the exchange may inaccurately reflect underlying supply and demand, and the prices on the exchange may also be more easily manipulated by a few large trades.

The government has said that these reforms will accelerate growth in the sector through private sector investment by building infrastructure and supply chains for farm produce in national and global markets. They are intended to help small farmers who do not have the means to either bargain for their produce to get a better price or invest in technology to improve the productivity of farms. NCDEX is already in place and what we need to do now is to spread the network of digital techniques and digital financial services amongst the farmers and educate them for efficient use of the same.

Endnotes

1. The practice by which a business or investor limits risk by taking positions that tends to offset each other.
2. https://ncdex.com/fpo/fpo-overview:

Agri-futures are financial contracts requiring the buyer to purchase an asset or the seller to sell a physical agri-commodity at a predetermined future date and price.

3. An exchange may facilitate efficient physical trade of a commodity or provide a venue for price risk management and speculation.

References

Francisco, Ceballos, Kanna, Samyuktha, Singh, Vartika and Kramer, Berber (2019), "Digital Technologies for Financial Inclusion of Smallholder Farmers", International Food Policy Research Institute.

https://gcgh.grandchallenges.org/challenge/smart-farming-innovations-small-scale-producers.

https://www.gpfi.org/sites/gpfi/files/documents/Digital%20Financial%20Inclusion-CompleteReport-Final-A4.pdf.

https://www.mckinsey.com/industries/agriculture/our-insights/how-digital-innovation-is-transforming-agriculture-lessons-from-india.

Kanitkar, A. and Prasad, C.S. (2019), "Farming Future: Emerging Social Enterprises in India".

Purohit, Pooja (2016), "Measurements of Regulations of the Agricultural Produce Markets", *Economic and Political Weekly.*

UNCTAD (2009), "Development Impacts of Commodity Exchanges in Emerging Markets".

USAID (2017), "Feed the Future Enabling Environment for Food Security: Assessing the Preconditions for Commodity Exchange Success", A Guidance Document.

3

Digital Financial Services and Their Impact on Financial Inclusion

Mohd. Shafeeq and Sana Beg

Digital Financial Inclusion in India

The committee on Financial Inclusion headed by Dr. C. Rangarajan defined financial inclusion as "the process of ensuring access to financial services and timely and adequate credit where needed by vulnerable groups such as weaker sections and low-income groups at an affordable cost". While the term digital financial inclusion is defined as "digital access to and use of formal financial services by excluded and underserved populations, such services should be suited to the customers' needs and delivered responsibly, at a cost both affordable to customers and sustainable for providers" (Lauer, Kate; Lyman, Timothy, 2015). In simple terms, digital financial inclusion refers to the process of achieving financial inclusion through digital means.

In 2014, men were 20 percentage points more likely than women to have an account, while after three years this gender gap shrank by 14 percentage points and reached 6 percentage points. This happened because of an increase in account ownership which was an outcome of biometric identification cards. Biometric identification cards have helped India in reducing the leakage of funds for pension payments by 47 percent. Also, the gap between the top 60 percent of adults from the richest households and the bottom 40 percent of the adults from the poorest households reduced from 15 percentage points to 5 percentage points due to government policies.

Globally, in 2017, there were 1.7 billion people who were unbanked and nearly half of them lived in Bangladesh, China, India, Indonesia, Mexico, Nigeria, and Pakistan. India roughly had an unbanked population of around 190 million. It must also be noted that in India, more than 50 percent of the unbanked population had a mobile phone, which is a pre-requisite for improving the status of digital financial inclusion in any given country. In India, around 65 million of the banked population used cash or over-the-counter service to send/receive remittances (World Bank Group, 2017).

It is believed that the status of financial inclusion will improve in India by using the technology because conventional banking (brick and mortar) is proving to be an extravagant proposition for banks in rural or remote areas and it is also not proving to be beneficial for low ticket size transactions. Additionally, distribution challenges in such areas, apart from lack of awareness about financial products, requirement of skilled and trained manpower and a high proportion of no-frill accounts are some other issues (KPMG, 2015). Government policies, regulations, and infrastructure play a prominent role in accelerating the role of fintech in enhancing the status of digital financial inclusion. For instance, goods and service tax (GST) and *Jan Dhan Yojana* have played an important role in establishing the footprints of fintech in the Indian market. While UPI, the Digital India programme, and availability of the internet are providing a robust infrastructure to digitalize the economy, policies like granting of the license to payment banks in India by the RBI, has also boosted digital financial status in India (ASSOCHAM, 2019).

Vital Components of Digital Financial Inclusion Model

As per the report of the CGAP (Consultative Group to Assist the Poor), there are three key components in digital financial inclusion model. These are:

Digital Transactional Platform: To understand this

component, let us first understand the situation when a buyer and seller meet at a geographical place where they can buy/sell their commodities. In the absence of these geographical platforms, both buyer and seller will have to face difficulty in settlements. Thus, geographical platforms act as facilitators in settlement and thus can be called as transactional platforms. Whenever such transactions are settled via virtual mode, the platform will be termed as the digital transactional platform. In the context of digital financial inclusion, this digital transactional platform is a summation of all those facilitators which support activities like remittances, storage of surplus wealth, payments, and receipts of the customers, duly built-in by the financial service providers. Facilitators in digital transactional platforms include a device, a digital communication channel, and a financial services provider (bank or non-bank who are allowed to store electronic value).

For instance, in India, both bank and non-bank providers are allowed to store electronic value. Banks will include those institutions which are licensed by the RBI while non-bank institutions will include those service providers who are not licensed by the RBI. For example, Paytm which was launched in the year 2010 as a platform for doing online transactions like pre-paid/post-paid recharges, booking railway tickets, etc, was later granted a license by the RBI to act as a payment bank in India and thus it became Paytm Payments Bank Ltd. in August 2015. Before August 2015, Paytm was a non-bank financial service provider but after obtaining the license of payment bank from the RBI, Paytm became a bank. Besides Paytm, 10 more companies received license from the RBI in 2015. At present six payment banks are operational in India, viz. Paytm Payments Bank Ltd., Airtel Payments Bank Ltd., FINO Payments Bank Ltd., India Post Payments Bank Ltd., Jio Payments Bank Ltd., and NSDL Payments Bank Ltd..

India currently has 22 private sector banks, 3 local area banks, 11 small finance banks, 6 payment banks, 12 public sector banks, 4 financial institutions, 43 regional rural banks, and 44 foreign banks. Non-bank providers will include those services provider who store money virtually, as for example, Amazon Pay etc.

Retail Agents: These are those individuals who have the device and are connected to a communication network with financial service providers. These agents have a device with them and whenever a customer approaches them either to convert cash into virtual money or to convert virtual money into cash, these agents then accordingly process the request of the customer.

Device: A device can be any digital means with the help of which information can be sent from customers to the retail agents and from retail agents to financial service providers. For example, using a mobile phone, customers can process the request with the retail agent and using a PoS (point of sale), terminal retail agents can process the request to the financial service provider.

Mobile Phones: From Table 3.1, it can be observed that there has been an overall rise in the tele-density from the year 2011-12 till 2019-20. Though in the past few years, India has been witnessing a fall in tele-density, yet its position in terms of telecom subscribers is very high. The figure is roughly revolving around 90 percent despite a fall in the tele-density ratio. The picture of the growth rate of telecom subscribers is much better in rural areas as compared to the urban areas.

Table 3.1: Growth of Telecom Subscribers and Tele-density in India: 2011-12 to 2019-20

(in million)

Year	Telecom subscribers	Urban	Rural	Growth of telecom subscribers (%)
2011-12	951.34	620.52	330.82	-
2012-13	898.02	548.80	349.22	-5.60
2013-14	933.00	555.26	377.73	3.90
2014-15	996.49	577.18	419.31	6.80
2015-16	1058.86	609.69	449.17	6.26
2016-17	1194.58	692.97	501.61	12.82
2017-18	1206.22	681.61	524.61	0.97
2018-19	1183.51	669.16	514.35	-1.88
2019-20	1177.97	656.46	521.51	-0.47

contd...

Year	Growth urban (%)	Growth rural (%)	Projected population	Tele-density* (%)
2011-12	-	-	1208.12	78.75
2012-13	-11.56	5.56	1223.58	73.39
2013-14	1.18	8.16	1238.89	75.31
2014-15	3.95	11.01	1254.02	79.46
2015-16	5.63	7.12	1268.96	83.44
2016-17	13.66	11.67	1283.60	93.06
2017-18	-1.64	4.59	1298.04	92.93
2018-19	-1.83	-1.96	1312.24	90.19
2019-20	-1.90	1.39	1326.16	88.83

* Calculated, dividing the number of telecom subscribers by projected population and multiplying the resultant with 100.
Source: Based on author's calculations (data obtained from TRAI and Census of India).

Various Digital Financial Services in India

National Payments Corporation of India (NPCI) was founded in the year 2008 with the objective of 'operating retail payments and settlements in India'. It is an initiative by the RBI (Reserve Bank of India) and IBA (Indian Banks Associations) under the provisions of the Payments and Settlement Systems Act, 2007. NPCI is a non-profit organization and maintains data regarding retail payments.

The data about the volume of various digital financial services, particularly in the retail sector, is given in Table 3.2, while data about their values is available in Table 3.3.

NPCI provides financial data on various digital financial services which includes; NFS Inter-Bank ATM Cash Withdrawal, NACH, CTS, IMPS, Rupay Card usage at PoS, Rupay Card usage at eCom, AEPS, BBPS, UPI, USSD 1.0, and NETC.

NFS (National Financial Switch) Inter-Bank ATM Cash Withdrawal is the largest network of shared automated teller machines (ATMs) in India. It is responsible for interconnecting the ATM network in India. It is managed by NPCI since December 2009.

National Automated Clearing House (NACH) is an electronic payment system that is implemented by NPCI to facilitate interbank, high volume, debit/credit transactions, which are bulky and are repetitive. This service is available for banks, financial institutions, corporate, and government departments.

Table 3.2: Volume of Digital Financial Services in India

(in million)

NPCI Operated Systems	2017-18	2018-19	2019-20
NFS Inter-Bank ATM cash withdrawal	3,503.44 (10.51)	4,017.41 (14.67)	4,311.59 (7.32)
NACH	2,375.33 (20.70)	2,861.38 (20.46)	3,401.77 (18.89)
CTS	1,138.06 (2.36)	1,112.07 (-2.28)	1,035.89 (-6.85)
IMPS	1,009.84 (99.24)	1,752.91 (73.58)	2,579.17 (47.14)
RuPay Card usage at (POS)	459.55 (135.40)	695.02 (51.24)	822.59 (18.35)
RuPay Card usage at (eCom)	208.11 (137.68)	432.06 (107.61)	658.13 (52.32)
AEPS	106.27 (552.36)	254.47 (139.46)	437.19 (71.80)
BBPS	10.6 (35,233)	73.5 (593.40)	145.69 (98.22)
UPI	915.23 (5024.47)	5,353.40 (484.92)	12,518.6 (133.84)
USSD 1.0	4.64 (-88.68)	-	-
NETC	126.52 (437.93)	254.03 (100.78)	582.59 (129.34)

Note: Figures given in the brackets represent growth rate (G). [2]
Source: NPCI, 2020.

Cheque Truncation System (CTS): It is a process that avoids physical movement of cheques from one bank to another. When a physical cheque is presented in the bank by the cheque holder, an electronic image of the cheque along with the MICR line of the cheque is forwarded to the payee bank. Payee bank on receiving the request processes the cheque for payment and thus this process helps in settling the payments between banks in a short period.

Immediate Payment Services (IMPS): It is a non-card retail payment service operated by National Payments Corporation of India (NPCI) in collaboration with member banks.

It is available 24x7. Under IMPS, beneficiary gets funds on a real time basis with the settlement between banks happening on a deferred net basis.

Table 3.3: Value of Digital Financial Services in India.

(in ₹ billion)

NPCI Operated Systems	2017-18	2018-19	2019-20
NFS Inter-Bank ATM cash Withdrawal	13,357.49 (23.47)	15,125.62 (13.24)	16,150.98 (6.78)
NACH	9,752.88 (35.31)	13,383.60 (37.23)	17,629.99 (31.73)
CTS	79,451.24 (7.32)	81,535.92 (2.62)	79,174.61 (-2.90)
IMPS	8,924.98 (116.82)	15,902.57 (78.18)	23,375.41 (46.99)
RuPay Card usage at (PoS)	488.23 (68.38)	808.23 (65.54)	1,146.81 (41.89)
RuPay Card usage at (eCom)	166.09 (179.90)	366.9 (120.90)	610.4 (66.37)
AEPS	269.17 (1079.54)	678.31 (152)	1,188.58 (75.23)
BBPS	10.98 (27350)	90.99 (728.69)	216.62 (138.07)
UPI	1,098.32 (1481)	8,769.70 (698.46)	21,317.30 (143.08)
USSD 1.0	0	-	-
NETC	33.39 (405.14)	57.38 (71.85)	112.94 (96.83)

Note: Figures given in brackets represent growth rate (G).
Source: NPCI, 2020.

Used mainly for remittances, IMPS has become popular in recent years. Lately, IMPS has been allowed for receiving foreign inward remittances also.

Currently, a majority of inter-bank mobile fund transfer transactions are channelised through NEFT mechanism. Under NEFT, the transactions are processed and settled in batches, hence are not real time. Also, the transactions can be done only during the working hours of the RTGS system.

In the above context, NPCI carried out a pilot project on mobile payment system initially with 4 member banks, viz. State

Bank of India, Bank of India, Union Bank of India and ICICI Bank in August 2010. Yes Bank, Axis Bank and HDFC Bank joined this pilot project in the months of September, October and November 2010 respectively. IMPS public launch happened on November 22, 2010 by Shrimati Shyamala Gopinath, DG RBI at Mumbai and this service is now available to the Indian public. As in September 2021, 644 entities were live members of IMPS which includes small finance banks, public sector banks, private banks, payment banks, RRBs, co-operative banks and PPIs.

IMPS offers instant, 24x7, inter-bank electronic funds transfer service through mobile phones. IMPS facilitates customers to use mobile instruments as a channel for accessing their bank accounts and put high inter-bank fund transfers in a secured manner with immediate confirmation features. This facility is provided by NPCI through its National Financial Switch (NFS).

The eligible criteria for the banks who can participate in IMPS is that the bank should have approval from the RBI for mobile banking service.

RuPay: RuPay is an Indian domestic card payment scheme conceived and launched by National Payments Corporation of India (NPCI). It aims to fulfil RBI's vision to offer a domestic, open-loop, multilateral system which will allow all Indian banks and financial institutions in India to participate in electronic payments.

"RuPay", the word itself has a sense of nationality in it. "RuPay" has the coinage of two terms viz. Rupee and payment. The RuPay visual identity is a modern and dynamic unit. The orange and green arrows indicate a nation on the move and a service that matches its pace. The colour blue stands for the feeling of tranquillity which people must get while owning card of the brand 'RuPay'. The bold and unique typeface grants solidity to the whole unit and symbolizes a stable entity.

RuPay was created to fulfil RBI's desire to have a domestic, open-loop, and multilateral system of payments in India. In India,

90 percent of credit card transactions and almost all debit card transactions are domestic. However, the cost of transactions was high due to the monopoly of foreign gateways like Visa and MasterCard. In recent years, the usage of credit and debit cards (called plastic money) has increased manifold. It was thought that if this process of transactions is made India-centric, cost can come down drastically. RuPay facilitates electronic payment at all Indian banks and financial institutions, and competes with MasterCard and Visa in India. NPCI maintains ties with Discover Financial to enable the card scheme to gain international acceptance.

RuPay card was launched on March 26, 2012. NPCI entered into a strategic partnership with Discover Financial Services (DFS) for RuPay Card, enabling the acceptance of RuPay Global Cards on Discover's global payment network outside of India.

RuPay cards are accepted at all ATMs across India under National Financial Switch, and under the NPCI's agreement with DFS, RuPay cards are also accepted on the international Discover network. All point-of-sale (PoS) terminals in India are under RuPay platform. To enable this, RuPay has certified major banks in India to accept RuPay cards at their respective PoS terminals located at different merchant locations. In addition to the ATMs and PoS terminals, RuPay cards are accepted online on e-commerce websites.

Aadhaar-enabled Payment System (AEPS): AEPS is a payment service offered by the National Payments Corporation of India (NPCI) to banks, financial institutions using Aadhaar card. AEPS is a bank-led model, which allows online financial inclusion transaction at micro-ATMs through business correspondents (BCs) of any bank using Aadhaar authentication. This system is designed to handle both ON-US (intra-bank) and OFF-US (inter-bank) requests seamlessly in an effective way by enabling authentication gateway for all Aadhaar-linked account holders.

It is a payment service empowering a bank customer to use

Aadhaar as his identity to access his respective Aadhaar-enabled bank account and perform basic banking transactions. It allows bank-to-bank transaction at PoS (micro-ATM). The user has to link his account with his Aadhar number at the bank. Users can do as many transactions at any AEPS point without any PIN or password. This service is meant to speed track financial inclusion in the country.

Unified Payments Interface (UPI): UPI is a system that powers multiple bank accounts into a single mobile application (of any participating bank), merging several banking features, seamless fund routing and merchant payments into one hood. It is a system for instant electronic payment through user's smart phone. It is an advanced version of immediate payment services (IMPS) which is used to transfer money between bank accounts. Like IMPS, UPI facilitates round-the-clock funds transfer service. It authenticates the identity of the user like a debit card, using the phone as a tool instead of a separate card. It works 24x7 and for 365 days.

One needs a smart phone with UPI application (app) and a bank account.

Present Status of Various Digital Financial Services in India in the Retail Sector

From the available statistics, it can be observed that there has been a continuous rise in the volume of various digital financial services in retail sector, maintained by the NPCI. A fall has been witnessed only in the volumes of CTS and USSD 1.0. While the value of various digital financial services exhibited a similar pattern like that of volumes, overall, there has been a continuous rise in the aggregate volume and value of all digital financial transactions of the retail sector. Financial year 2018-19 witnessed the highest growth rate in aggregate volume of all digital financial services (70.49 percent), while the least growth rate of 32.04 percent was recorded in financial year 2016-17. Between 2016-17 and 2018-19, growth rate of the aggregate volume of financial transactions also increased. Aggregate value of all financial transactions conducted by NPCI continuously increased and growth rate of the aggregate value also witnessed a rise between 2014-15 and 2018-19. The highest growth rate (20.40 percent) in the aggregate value was recorded in the financial year 2018-19, while the year 2015-16 witnessed the lowest growth rate of 12.03 percent.

Amongst all the financial services in the retail sector offered by NPCI, UPI and NETC were the only services that recorded a growth rate of over 100 percent in all the financial years in terms of volume. In terms of value, UPI stands out in the picture, as it recorded a rise of over 100 percent in all the financial years studied here.

Various new digital financial services have been offered by the NPCI during the last 5 to 6 years. These services include Rupay cards, AEPS, BBPS, UPI, USSD 1.0, and NETC. Data for AEPS were made available from 2015-16 while for BBPS, UPI, USSD 1.0, and NETC, it was made available from 2016-17.

This clearly indicates that India is striving hard towards 'Digital India' initiative as NPCI is offering a variety of financial services in the retail sector. For instance, BBPS allows customers to make bill payments at one place, while UPI offers customers to create their own unique UPI id that can be used to easily pay or receive funds either directly to the UPI connected bank account or by scanning the QR code, making receipts and payments much easier in comparison to the traditional modes of NEFT/RTGS. NFS has helped in reducing the cost by minimizing capital requirements of banks. NACH has helped banks, financial institutions, corporate and government departments to make payments easily that are bulky and repetitive. CTS had reduced the time of settlements. IMPS had provided the convenience to use it 24x7x365. RuPay card is catering to the needs of Indian markets. NETC is helping in handling the toll collection by the respective governments and AEPS has brought inclusiveness, as people can withdraw their money using the biometric Aadhar authentication.

This diversified set of financial services is proving beneficial for the country as can be witnessed from the respective growth rates of these services, though some of these services are still in their infancy. However, concerted efforts are still required by the Government of India and the RBI to further their outreach. The only digital financial service that got discontinued is USSD 1.0 as this service now comes under the ambit of UPI and is now available as USSD 2.0 which offers the same services as USSD 1.0. Besides USSD 2.0, UPI also includes BHIM (Bharat Interface for Money), an application that is used to make a quick and easy transaction using the UPI.

NEFT and RTGS

Table 3.4 depicts data about NEFT (National Electronic Funds Transfer) and RTGS (Real Time Gross Settlement). Since 2011, the volume and value of NEFT and RTGS has been rising continuously, though the year 2019 witnessed a slower growth rate in value terms regards NEFT (7.68 percent) while in the case of RTGS (2.48 percent) it was witnessed in the year 2014. Overall, the status of NEFT and RTGS has been satisfactory in India.

Mobile Banking

Table 3.5 displays data about mobile banking in India. Amongst all the digital financial services (including the digital financial services in the retail sector managed by NPCI or the digital financial services that are managed by NPCI and RBI), mobile banking is the only digital financial service that has shown remarkable growth in terms of both volume and value. Since the inception of mobile banking in India (2009), it can be observed from Table 3.5 that the volume and value of mobile banking has seen an upward mobility.

M-Pesa of Kenya

It is quite clear that India is witnessing an alarming growth rate in mobile banking in particular, and it is also evident from the experience of other developing countries like Kenya, who have managed to improve their financial inclusion index through the use of M-Pesa. In Kenya, M-Pesa was launched in the year 2007 by Safaricom and the regulatory environment played an important role in its success. The Central Bank of Kenya offered a 'no objection' certificate to Safaricom that allowed the company to pilot test their services without any strict regulations.

Table 3.4: NEFT/RTGS Growth Rates in India

(volume in million and value in ₹ billion)

Year	NEFT			
	Volume	G (%)	Value	G (%)
2011	199.48	-	15377	-
2012	339.62	70.25	25887	68.35
2013	571.86	68.38	39919	54.20
2014	873.03	52.66	55339	38.63
2015	1161.92	33.09	75985	37.31
2016	1480.77	27.44	106103	39.64
2017	1897.65	28.15	157997	48.91
2018	2218.09	16.89	216347	36.93
2019	2621.74	18.20	232966	7.68
Year	**RTGS**			
	Volume	**G (%)**	**Value**	**G (%)**
2011	51.11	-	519375	-
2012	65.47	28.10	644714	24.13
2013	78.09	19.28	725983	12.61
2014	89.9	15.12	743993	2.48
2015	97.27	8.20	794160	6.74
2016	103.17	6.07	943727	18.83
2017	120.94	17.22	1107988	17.41
2018	134.57	11.27	1284601	15.94
2019	148.23	10.15	1388669	8.10

contd...

Calculated by the authors

Source: https://www.rbi.org.in/scripts/NEFTUserView.aspx?Id=148.

The success story of Safaricom was well supported by the existing conditions in the country, as in 2008 there was political violence which led to the disruption of traditional banking services and to send/receive money, and Safaricom was the only available option at that time and also financial services were absent for remittances. This situation gave a favourable boost to Safaricom and this helped the company in establishing its presence in Kenya (European Investment Bank, 2014).

Table 3.5: Mobile Banking Growth Rate in India

(volume in million and value in ₹ billion)

Year	Mobile Banking			
	Volume	G (%)	Value	G (%)
2009	0.76	-	0.53	-
2010	5.04	563.16	4.53	754.717
2011	19.26	282.14	14.1	211.2583
2012	44.68	131.98	41.85	196.8085
2013	83.00	85.77	161.93	286.9295
2014	144.61	74.23	666.25	311.4432
2015	308.46	113.30	2862.59	329.657
2016	798.58	158.89	10288.9	259.4266
2017	1509.3	89.00	15466.7	50.32399
2018	4555.08	201.80	22840.5	47.67507
2019	11997.8	163.39	52549.5	130.0721

Calculated by the authors

Source: https://www.rbi.org.in/scripts/NEFTUserView.aspx?Id=148.

Many factors have contributed to the success of Safaricom in Kenya including the following:

1. High level of *literacy rates* (more than 85 percent).
2. Favourable *regulatory environment* offered by the Central Bank of Kenya.
3. More than 83 percent of the population in Kenya, over the age of 15 years, is familiar with the basic operations of mobile phones, thus conditions for *technology adoption* were favourable.
4. Productive *marketing campaign* was run by Safaricom to boost the use of M-Pesa in Kenya.
5. Low level of *the competitive environment*.

Above mentioned factors contributed favourably in increasing the use of digital financial services in Kenya which in turn enhanced their position in terms of digital financial inclusion. In the context of India, it can be said that products are widely available [3], mobile penetration (88.83 percent) [4] is high, literacy rate is high of (77.77 percent) [5], and access to finance is high (90 percent). [6] November 2016 was the year in which demonetization was announced in India which gave a push to the use of digital financial services [7]. A year later the implementation of goods and service tax (GST) took place which helped the Indian economy bring the unorganized sector within the ambit of the organized sector through GST and also created the demand for the establishments of various fintech services in India (ASSOCHAM, 2019). COVID-19 pandemic has further pushed the economy towards digitalization in a short period of time (PWC, 2020). These three series of events have been catalyst in pushing the Indian economy towards digitalization.

Thus, it can be said that these events have led to an increase in *demand* for various digital financial services. RBI has been working diligently towards achieving higher financial inclusion through digitalization which in turn will improve digital financial inclusion in India. To achieve this goal, RBI has launched various policy measures like e-KYC, granting of license to payment banks, allowing interoperability [8] and launch of new digital financial services like UPI, BHIM, etc.

Such measures undertaken by RBI prove that *the regulatory environment* is favourable in India towards the use of digital financial services. Based on the data of the Telecom Regulatory Authority of India (TRAI) (Table 3.1), it can be said that *technology adoption* is satisfactory in India and there has been a high rate of tele-density in the country. To further push digitalization in the economy, marketing campaign are being rigorously pursued by various financial players in the country. For instance, Paytm is spreading digital awareness via the marketing campaign, *Join the Revolution! Teach everyone around you to pay and accept payments using Paytm. 10,000 lucky winners will receive INR 2,100 and 1 lakh winners will get certificates"* (Paytm, 2019). Kotak Mutual Funds launched a campaign to promote SIP (Systematic Investment Plan) in 2020. ICICI Bank and Policy Bazaar have also been advertising to sell policies online. Thus, productive *marketing campaign* is on the run in India to increase the use of various digital financial services.

India currently has 22 private sector banks, 3 local area banks, 11 small finance banks, 6 payment banks, 12 public sector banks, 4 financial institutions, 43 regional rural banks, and 44 foreign banks, to provide financial services online and offline and even through business correspondents (BCs)—a robust *ecosystem* for promoting digital financial services. If we talk only about payment banks, then 6 such banks are competing to grab their share in digital financial services. Thus there are a very low number of competitors, who are only operating virtually and competing for their digital financial service share. Thus, it can be said that in India there is a moderate degree of *competition* amongst the digital financial service providers.

After reviewing all the factors that contributed to the success of Safaricom in Kenya, for India, it can be said that all the factors have depicted similar characteristics in India in comparison to Kenya except in the case of competitors. In Kenya, Safaricom was the only digital financial service provider while in India there are more than one digital financial service providers. Undoubtedly, the increased competition will help in spreading digitalization at a rapid pace.

Despite favourable conditions for improving the status of digital financial inclusion in India, the goal seems a bit far but not unreachable. It is because of the presence of a large bunch of unbanked population which was 190 million in 2017. India is at the second position when it comes to unbanked population, with China being at the top (World Bank Group, 2017). Secondly, women are overrepresented among the unbanked population in India (World Bank Group, 2017). Thirdly, the gender gap in account ownership—though the gap was reduced from 20 percentage point in 2014 to 6 percentage point in 2017 (World Bank Group, 2018).

Thus, to achieve a higher degree of digital financial inclusion in India, the Government has to focus on reducing the gender gap in account ownership, uplifting the status of digital financial inclusion in urban as well as rural areas, creating newer employment opportunities, reducing poverty, educating people about the use of digital financial services, increasing GDP, focussing on those states/Union Territories (UTs) where the status of financial inclusion is low, matching the demand and supply of digital financial services and promoting digital literacy and awareness.

Endnotes

1. Magnetic ink character recognition (MICR) is a type of code that is printed on the cheque.
2. 'G' here refers to the growth rate which is calculated by subtracting the value of the previous year from the next successive year and then dividing the result by the value of the previous year and later multiplying it by 100.
3. Based on the types of digital financial services offered by RBI and NPCI.
4. Data released by TRAI on tele-density, including mobile phones.
5. Based on NSS 75th Round, it can be said that there is high literacy rate in India (77.77 percent) [National Statistical Office (NSO), 2020], though in Kenya literacy rate was over 85 percent.
6. As per the World Bank's Global Findex Database, 2017, it can be said that there is a higher rate of access to finance because 80 percent of the population has a bank account (World Bank Group, 2017).
7. As per the report of the Reserve Bank of India (RBI), demonetization led to a sharp increase in the use of digital transactions (RBI, 2017) and also there was a rise in transactions by 62 percent at Paytm in the month December 2016. The report also suggested that demonetization may have led to an increase in digital financial transactions in India in a short period, but with the availability of cash, demonetization does not seem to have had a long-term impact on digital transactions.
8. In simple terms, it is a feature that allows a payment system to be used with other payment systems. It allows service issuer, service

provider, and service receiver, who are participants in different systems to clear and easily settle their payment transactions, without the need to enter into multiple systems (RBI, 2018).

References

ASSOCHAM (2019), "Emerging Technologies Disrupting the Financial Sector", available at: https://www.pwc.in/assets/pdfs/consulting/financial-services/fintech/publications/emerging-technologies-disrupting-the-financial-sector.pdf.

European Investment Bank (ed.) (2014), "Digital Financial Services in Africa: Beyond the Kenyan Success Story", European Investment Bank (EIB), Regional Studies and Roundtables, Luxembourg, available at: https://www.econstor.eu/bitstream/10419/113903/1/820291498.pdf.

Fhi360 (2019), "India Digital Financial Inclusion: Journey Map Report", available at: https://www.fhi360.org/sites/default/files/media/documents/resource-mstar-india-digital-financial-inclusion-report.pdf.

IFC (2009), "M-Money Channel Distribution Case: Kenya", available at: https://www.ifc.org/wps/wcm/connect/e0d2a9bd-16b9-4a36-8498-0b2650b9af8b/Tool%2B6.7.%2BCase%2BStudy%2B-%2BM-PESA%2BKenya%2B.pdf?MOD=AJPERES&CVID=jkCVy-n.

Inc 42 Media (2015), "Paytm Alongwith 10 Others Receive License from RBI to Set Up Payments Banks", available at: https://inc42.com/buzz/rbi-selects-11-companies-to-set-up-payments-bank.

KPMG (2015), "Role of Digital Banking in Furthering Financial Inclusion", available at: https://assets.kpmg/content/dam/kpmg/pdf/2015/08/Financial-Sector-POV.pdf.

Lauer, Kate and Lyman, Timothy (2015), "Digital Financial Inclusion: Implications for Customers, Regulators, Supervisors, and Standard-Setting Bodies", available at: https://www.cgap.org/sites/default/files/researches/documents/Brief-Digital-Financial-Inclusion-Feb-2015.pdf.

National Statistical Office (NSO) (2020), "Household Social

Consumption on Education in India", NSS 75th Round, available at:
http://www.mospi.gov.in/sites/default/files/publication_reports/Report_585_75th_round_Education_final_1507_0.pdf.

NPCI (n.d.), "RuPay Product Overview", available at: https://www.npci.org.in/product-overview/rupay-product-overview.

NPCI (n.d.), "UPI Product Overview", available at: https://www.npci.org.in/product-overview/upi-product-overview.

Paytm (2019), "Marketing Campaign", available at: https://paytm.com/offer/marketing-campaign.

Rangarajan, C. (2008), "Report of the Committee on Financial Inclusion", Reserve Bank of India, Mumbai.

RBI (2016), "Withdrawal of Legal Tender Status for ₹ 500 and ₹ 1000 Notes: RBI Notice", available at: https://rbidocs.rbi.org.in/rdocs/PressRelease/PDFs/PR114293ABB8ED55DA40ED8C80E7800CD47FDE.PDF.

RBI (2017), "Macroeconomic Impact of Demonetisation: A Preliminary Assessment", available at: https://rbidocs.rbi.org.in/rdocs/Publications/PDFs/MID10031760E85BDAFEFD497193995BB1B6DBE602.PDF.

RBI (2018), "Prepaid Payment Instruments (PPIs): Guidelines for Interoperability", available at: https://rbidocs.rbi.org.in/rdocs/notification/PDFs/NOTI61724025FD07FE407D8796EC6C97A17A8E.PDF.

Reserve Bank of India (n.d.), "Websites of Banks in India", available at:
https://www.rbi.org.in/:
https://www.rbi.org.in/scripts/banklinks.aspx.

Sarma, M. (2008), "Index of Financial Inclusion", Working Paper No. 215, Indian Council for Research on International Economic Relations.

TRAI (2020), "Telecom Subscriptions Reports", available at: https://www.trai.gov.in/release-publication/reports/telecom-subscriptions-reports.

Worl Bank (2018), "The Global Findex Database", International Bank for Reconstruction and Development, Washington D.C.

World Bank (2017), "Measuring Financial Inclusion and Fintech Revolution", Global Findex Database, available at:

https://globalfindex.worldbank.org/sites/globalfindex/files/2018-04/2017%20Findex%20full%20report_0.pdf.

4

Digital Green Finance and Sustainable Development

Manasi Gore

Need for Green Finance

Climate change is a serious global environmental concern, which is primarily caused by the building up of greenhouse gases in the atmosphere. Recent discourse on climate change has underscored the fact that climate change occupies a high priority on the environmental agenda of international community.

Global climate change due to rising levels of green house gases (GHGs) in the atmosphere is one of the most serious environmental concerns of present time. The accumulated scientific evidence clearly indicates that if the rate of GHG emissions is not reduced very significantly, there will be a damaging effect on the global climate.

Since global warming is caused by total accumulation of GHG and each country's emissions add to the stock, the cost of each country's emissions is borne by the entire global community. Similarly, the benefits of reduction in emission by any one country accrue not to the country itself but to the entire global community. This is classically a situation characterized by externalities in which individual countries will not have a sufficient incentive to undertake mitigation unless all countries co-operate in what is felt to be a collective effort with an equitable distribution of the burden of reducing emissions.

The Intergovernmental Panel on Climate Change (IPCC), established in 1988 by the World Meteorological Organization (WMO) and the United Nations Environment Programme

(UNEP), has worked extensively on evaluating past trends and the future prospects of climate change. IPCC reviews and assesses the most recent scientific, technical, and socio-economic information produced worldwide relevant to climate change.

According to IPCC, the global temperature may rise by 2-4.5 degree centigrade by the end of this century, including a 2.7-4.3°C increase over India by 2080s if adequate actions are not taken to reduce emissions globally. At the national level, the observed increase in surface air temperatures over the past century is 0.4 degree centigrade.

The change in the climate system is likely to have adverse impact on the economy, livelihoods, cropping pattern, and food security. According to the various projections by the IPCC, extreme heat events are likely to be longer and more intense in addition to changes in precipitation patterns. The change in climate could: (a) affect the production of wheat, rice, and maize in the tropical and temperate zones, (b) have negative impact on health by exacerbating health problems that already exist especially in developing countries, and (c) adversely impact productive activities like growing food and working outdoors.

The ecological overshoot problem, i.e. the ecological footprint being larger than the bio-capacity of the population, is an important issue in the global climate discourse. The *overshoot* can also be understood in terms of the carbon budget. The risk of climate change is largely a function of total cumulative GHGs in the atmosphere. IPCC AR5 has estimated that for temperature increase to remain below 2°C of pre-industrial levels the world can emit only about 2,900 giga tonnes (Gt) of CO_2 from all sources from the industrial revolution till 2100.

Till 2011, the world has emitted 1,900 Gt of CO_2, thus already consuming around two-thirds of this budget. This means that out of the budget of 2,900 Gt, only 1,000 Gt remains to be used between now and 2100. The World Resources Institute estimates that if emissions continue unabated, the remaining budget will last only 30 more years.

The key issue, therefore, for designing emission reduction commitment is how this remaining sparse carbon budget should be allocated between countries in a manner which is both fair and achievable. This certainly should involve an assessment of historic responsibility based on how countries have contributed to cumulative emissions so far.

India's contribution to cumulative global CO_2 (1850-2011) was a meagre 3 percent as against 21 percent by the USA and 18 percent by the EU. The sustainability of the world economic system also needs to be analysed through the lens of social justice and equity. For developing countries, their future commitment will also be determined by what kind and level of financial, capacity-building, and other support is provided by developed countries that have contributed most to cumulative global GHG emissions so far.

There are multiple mitigation pathways that are likely to limit warming to below 2°C relative to pre-industrial levels. These pathways would require substantial emissions reduction over the next few decades and near zero emissions of CO_2 and other long-lived GHGs by the end of the century. Implementing such reductions poses substantial technological, economic, social, and institutional challenges.

Green Growth

Green growth involves rethinking growth strategies with regard to their impact on environmental sustainability and the environmental resources available to poor and vulnerable groups. It is significant to note that many stimulus packages announced globally to combat recession incorporated a green component. International experience is that green growth promotes inclusivity. Further, the renewable energy sector is relatively labour-intensive, with the potential for generating more jobs than the oil and gas industries.

Environment must not be considered as just another sector of national development. It should form a crucial guiding dimension for plans and programmes in each sector. This becomes clear only if the concern for environmental protection is understood in its proper context. Ecological degradation compromises the quality of life in the long-run.

Low-carbon green growth is a pattern of development that decouples economic growth from carbon emissions, pollution and resource use, and promotes growth through the creation of new environment-friendly products, industries and business models that also improve people's quality of life. Thus, low-carbon green growth entails the following:

1. Using less energy, improving the efficiency with which resources are used and moving to low-carbon energy sources.
2. Protecting and promoting the sustainable use of natural resources such as forests and peat lands.
3. Designing and disseminating low-carbon technologies and business models to reinvigorate local economies.
4. Implementing policies and incentives which discourage carbon intensive practices.

Green growth is not anti-growth. Rather, it represents a change in how we manage economies to reflect a broader conception of what constitutes effective and sustainable growth. Environmental assets—water, land, air, ecosystems and the services they provide—represent a significant share of a country's wealth. Just like physical and human capital, natural capital requires investment, maintenance, and good management if it is to be productive and fully contribute to prosperity.

Green growth requires policies that are on their own terms good for growth, as well as for the environment, such as reforming energy subsidies or trade barriers that protect pollution-intensive sectors. It entails politically difficult reforms in the patterns of pricing, regulation, and public investment, and calls for complex changes in behaviours and social norms. Importantly, green growth requires knowing when to go for the politically expedient rather than the economically optimal.

Digital Green Finance

According to the United Nations Environment Programme (UNEP), green financing is to increase the level of financial flows (from banking, micro credit, insurance and investment) from the public, private and not-for-profit sectors to sustainable development priorities. A key part of this is to better manage environmental and social risks, take up opportunities that bring both a decent rate of return and environmental benefit and deliver greater accountability.

According to the Global Green Finance Index (GGFI), "green finance refers to any financial instrument or financial services activity—including insurance, equity, bonds, commodity and derivatives trading, analytical or risk management tools—which results in positive change for the environment and society over the long-term (sustainability). The most basic "greenness" criterion of a company or project is that it contributes to reduce green house gas emissions. Green finance is no longer seen as a fringe activity, but a profitable and desirable activity, which drives financial markets, serves society and enhances the status of financial centres which demonstrate expertise".

The Green Finance Study Group (GSFG) defines "green finance" as financing of investments that provide environmental benefits in the broader context of environmentally sustainable development. These environmental benefits include reductions in air, water and land pollution, reductions in greenhouse gas (GHG) emissions, improved energy efficiency while utilizing existing natural resources, and the mitigation of and adaptation to climate change. Green finance aims to internalize environmental externalities in order to boost environmentally friendly investments and reduce environmentally harmful ones.

It is a core part of low carbon green growth as it connects financial framework, environmental improvement and economic growth. When this finance is enabled with an ecosystem of technologies, such as artificial intelligence (AI) and big data, that is web-based and on the mobile platforms, distributed through the internet of things (IoT), in other words when the Green finance is digitized, it is known as the digital green finance. According to the PwC, AI could lift global GDP by US$ 15-20 trillion and is expected to annually connect an average of 125 billion devices worldwide by 2030.

The digital green finance would thus connect the mainstream financial system by adopting new technologies and finance innovations combined with Sustainable Development Goals (SDGs). Of the 17 SDGs outlined by the UNDP, digital green finance has direct first order connection to almost 12 goals like No Poverty (Goal 1), Access to Clean Water and Sanitation (Goal 6), Access to Affordable and Clean Energy (Goal 7), Reducing Inequality (Goal 10), Sustainable Consumption and Production (Goal 12) and so on. Also, it has a second order/indirect connection to some of these SDGs like Access to Healthcare (Goal 3), Sustainable Cities and Communities (Goal 11) and so on. This linkage of the digital green finance and the SDGs strongly build a case for digital green finance globally and for India particularly. The main stakeholders of digital green finance are as under:

1. Government with its regulatory framework, institutional set-up and subsidies/tax incentives and so on.
2. Business units like banks, insurance companies, institutional investors, MNCs, micro credit institutions with their financial instruments, products, technology, innovations, management and the forward and backward linkages.
3. Citizens who are aware and willing to pay for environment-friendly lifestyles.

International Finance Corporation (IFC) estimates cumulative climate investment potential of US$ 29.4 trillion across six key sectors in emerging market cities through 2030. These sectors include waste, renewable energy, public transportation, climate-smart water, electric vehicles, and green buildings. As per the Green Finance Mapping Report, 2019 of International Development Finance Club (IDFC), since 2015, cumulatively, nearly US$ 670 billion had been mobilized worldwide as green finance of which 78 percent was from the IDFC members (SIDBI is the member from India). Of these, 79 percent went to green energy and mitigation of green house gases (GHGs).

In 2018, the total green finance was US$ 134 billion, of which, climate finance constituted US$ 125 billion consisting of all activities related to mitigation of GHG emissions and adaptation to climate change and it accounted for 93 percent of total green finance. Finance for green energy and mitigation of GHGs was the largest category, representing 85 percent of climate finance. Remaining 7 percent of the green finance went to other environmental finance, which includes waste and water management, biodiversity, and controlling industrial pollution. The share of total green finance commitments made in the home country of the relevant IDFC member institutions was 78 percent (US$ 104 billion of the total (US$ 134 billion), while 22 percent (US$ 30 billion) was spent internationally.

In the total green finance, the share of East Asia and Pacific region was the largest at around 56 percent of which India was a leading country. The data implies growth of green finance worldwide and India is not an exception to it. Banks and other financial institutions in India started going green following their sense of growing awareness about climate change mitigation and introduction of new green finance instruments and/or products, listed below.

Green Loans and Mortgages

Loans given for a project or business that is considered environmentally sustainable is a green loan. Green mortgage is a type of mortgage that provides a money-saving discount or a bigger loan for making energy-efficient improvements such as for buying a home that meets specific energy-efficiency standards e.g. green buildings norms.

Green finance includes both debt and equity investments. It is a source of long-term funding to help close financing gaps and mobilize capital for sustainable development, mainly in emerging economies like India. Green bonds are fixed income instruments whose proceeds are earmarked exclusively for new and existing projects with environmental benefits, specially focused on renewables, energy efficiency, water, clean transport, and climate change mitigation and adaptation. It is widely acknowledged now that green bonds is one of the main green finance instruments in practice, to deliver climate goals agreed at COP 21 (Paris Conference). India's share in green bonds was highlighted by Economic Survey, 2019-20, while stating, "India has become the second-largest market globally for Green bonds with US$ 10.3 billion worth of transactions in the first half of 2019, as issuers and investors continued to adopt policies and strategies linked to sustainable development goals".

Green Bonds

The movement that started in Sweden in 2007 resulted in the beginning of a new era for the issue of green bonds by the World Bank. As per the World Bank Report, 2019, issuance of green bonds resulted in growing awareness amongst the investors about the challenges of climate change that could be tackled with effective and rewarding green investments through the so called green bonds.

To specify, green bonds are debt securities issued by financial, non-financial or public entities where the proceeds are used to finance 100 percent green projects and assets. India now has the second-largest emerging green bonds market after China. Though the green bonds represent a smaller fraction of the over US$ 100 trillion of bonds outstanding globally, they indeed represent a significant market opportunity for investors seeking to align their investment strategies with environmental considerations. In the emerging markets, China remained the largest emerging market issuer, as well as the second largest issuer of green bonds globally. The largest volumes were registered by India, followed by Chile, Poland, the Philippines,

United Arab Emirates, and Brazil. The top ten emerging markets, regards green bond issuance in 2019, are listed in Table 4.1.

Table 4.1: Top Ten Green Bonds Markets (2019)

Countries	Volume (in US$ million)
China	34,338
India	3,195
Poland	2,924
Philippines	1,498
United Arab Emirates	1,270
Brazil	1,258
Czech Republic	832
Indonesia	750
Thailand	734
South Africa	724

Source: IFC Global Macro and Market Research, Bloomberg, Dealogic, Environmental Finance, Climate Bonds Initiative.

The green bonds market that started just five years back has exhibited tremendous potential so far, with a coupon rate (rate of return) ranging between 4.7 percent (foreign issuance) and 7.5 percent (domestic issuance). This difference resulted in over-subscription of green bonds issue of Indian Renewable Energy Development Agency Limited (IREDA) in 2016 by 5.1 times. The size of this issue ranged between US$ 100 million and up to US$ 1 billion. Looking at the smaller investment potential for multiple small investors, the small-sized green bonds issues stand ground due to their large size. This gets proved by the figures too as the issue size of less than US$ 500 million accounts for almost 96 percent of the total issuance.

The potential for green bond issuance depends on some key determinants such as the existence and quality of sustainable finance policies and regulatory support frameworks, the stage of capital market development, strong governance, and political stability. For the effective growth of this market, in January 2016, the Securities and Exchange

Board of India (SEBI) published its official green bonds requirements for Indian issuers making India the second country (after China) to provide national level guidelines. As per these guidelines, a debt security shall be considered 'green' if the funds raised through issuance of the debt securities are utilized for projects and/or assets falling under any of the following broad categories:

1. Renewable and sustainable energy including wind, solar, bio-energy, other sources of energy which use clean technology etc.
2. Clean transportation including mass/public transportation etc.
3. Sustainable water management including clean and/or drinking water, water recycling, etc.
4. Climate change adaptation.
5. Energy efficiency including efficient and green buildings etc.
6. Sustainable waste management including recycling, waste-to-energy, efficient disposal of wastage, etc.
7. Sustainable land use including sustainable forestry and agriculture, afforestation, etc.
8. Biodiversity conservation.

If we look at the use of proceeds of green bonds in India, the link between digital green finance in terms of green bonds and sustainable development becomes quite apparent.

In addition to the above mentioned regulatory frameworks and government initiatives regards awareness about climate change mitigation and related options, it is imperative to look at the Global Green Finance Index (GGFI), 2020. This Report identified 135 factors under 4 headings (infrastructure factors, business factors, human capital factors and sustainability factors, each having sub-factors viz. 15, 35, 45 and 40 respectively) across depth and quality of 120 financial centres globally. It is interesting to note here the rankings of three financial centres in India namely Mumbai, Gujarat and New Delhi.

Despite these impressive facts, the path forward for green bonds in particular and digital green finance in general, has many hurdles. Some of them are listed on next page.

1. Green bonds, being a relatively new type of investment and financial instrument, are perceived as high risk.
2. Lack of awareness about credit enhancement measures.
3. Limited role of the NBCs despite a huge potential.
4. Green bonds are more focussed on the renewable energy sector. There is still a large untapped potential for green bonds in sectors such as water, agriculture, forestry, waste, and land, which needs public intervention to make them attractive.
5. Exchanges are institutions which can facilitate a robust green bond market. India's Bombay Stock Exchange (BSE), the oldest and the largest stock exchange, established the country's first international exchange called the India INX in 2017. India needs to accelerate this at a rapid rate along with other financial market developments.
6. A major challenge is to ensure and maintain the quality of Indian green bonds, to capture a larger market globally.
7. India has issued 'Green Bond Guidelines' but do not yet have a project evaluation index to differentiate high green impact projects from the ones with a low impact.

To conclude, India has a great potential in digital green finance and the government through its various entities, is already boosting the market by participating in it and issuing green bonds. However, to attract people to this relatively new avenue of digital green finance, certain concessions, including tax exemptions need to be extended. Institutions like SIDBI and NABARD with their rural outreach can better attract the rural segment for these types of financial instruments. This would pave the way for economic development through more sustainable ways and would help in internalizing the negative externalities regards the anthropogenic effects on climate change.

References

Amundi Asset Management and International Finance Corporation (2019), "Emerging Market Green Bonds Report".

Gudrun, Rumpf (2019), "A Decade of Green Bonds: Origin, Present and Future".

IFC (2018), "Climate Investment Opportunities in Cities: An IFC Analysis", IFC Report, 2019, 'Green Buildings: A Finance and Policy Blueprint for Emerging Markets'.

Mani, M., Bandyopadhyay, S., Chonabayashi, S., Markandya, A. and Mosier, T. (2018), "South Asia's Hotspots: Impacts of Temperature and Precipitation Changes on Living Standards", The World Bank, available at: https://openknowledge.worldbank.org/handle/10986/28723.

PwC (2017), "Sizing the Prize", available at: https://www.pwc.com/gx/en/issues/analytics/assets/pwc-ai-analysis-sizing-the-prize-report.pdf.

Reserve Bank of India (2019), "Report on Trend and Progress of Banking in India, 2018-2019", available at: https://rbidocs.rbi.org.in/rdocs/Publications/PDFs/0RTP241219FL760D9F69321B47988DE44D68D9217A7E.PDF.

TERI (The Energy and Resources Institute) (n.d.), "Unlocking the Green Bond Potential in India", New Delhi.

5

Crypto Currency

Rajesh Mohapatra

Over a decade ago, the birth of Bitcoin sparked a revolution within the digital world and in 2021 the number of active crypto currencies has jumped to over 6,500, worldwide. Crypto currencies have now evolved past simple digital currencies, offering solutions to satisfy the complex needs of recent financial markets. Graphics from Abra visualizes the complex, ever-evolving crypto currency ecosystem and its real world applications. A crypto currency is a type of digital token that relies on cryptography for chaining together digital signatures of token transfers, peer-to-peer networking and decentralization. In some cases, a proof of work scheme is used to create and manage the currency.

What is Crypto Currency?

Crypto currency is a class of privately issued digital means of payment that depends predominantly on cryptography and distributed ledger technology (DLT) such as the block chain. A block chain is a continuous ledger in which transactions are stored as blocks and linked using cryptography. Crypto currency is often allotted through initial coin offerings (ICOs), which are used as a means for raising capital through crowd-funding. Crypto currency typically has some monetary characteristics, but is not a liability of any entity and is not backed by any authority. Its value is driven by users' confidence in it. This, coupled with limited supply, makes its value highly volatile and, therefore, not a reliable medium of exchange or store of value.

Characteristics of Crypto Currencies

Why are crypto currencies important in the long-run in context of digital finance?

1. **Borderless:** Drastically reduces fees and processing time, thanks to scarcity of cross-border restrictions.
2. **Censorship Free:** Prevents governments or major institutions from blocking financial activities at whim.
3. **Greater Financial Control:** Individuals can have total control of their funds.
4. **Greater Security:** Prevents fraudulent alterations from third parties.
5. **Lower Costs:** Lower transaction fees, thanks to fewer third parties.
6. **Greater Accessibility:** Reduces or eliminates traditional barriers to capital markets.

Much like web, which has forever altered how we live and work, crypto currencies have the potential to vary how people participate in global financial markets.

Categorizing the New Crypto Economy

Today's crypto currencies go beyond replacing cash. This new token-based economy is evolving with unique solutions emerging in finance, security, identification, social engagement, and ownership.

Crypto currencies are generally categorized by their primary application within the ecosystem.

1. **Payments:** Digital cash is often used for both e-commerce and brick-and-mortar retailers.
2. **Store of Value:** New sort of scarce native currency and a way of settlement.
3. **Programmable Money:** Borderless money that enables easy conversion between currencies.
4. **Stable Coins:** Crypto version of fiat which is tied to the worth of resources like gold or U.S. dollar.
5. **Privacy:** Private digital transactions, with some offering anonymity.

6. **Digital Ownership:** Digital handling, storage, and monetization of data.
7. **Decentralized Utilities:** Crypto-enabled networks, products, and services that exchange between assets.
8. **Alternative Finance:** Digital assets like collectibles, commodities, and tokenized securities. Crypto currencies are adding both value and utility to the digital economy and to the worldwide financial market in entirety.
9. **Applications of Crypto Currencies:** Because crypto currencies are programmable with customizable code, developers can design and adapt themselves for multiple uses within the digital economy.

Use in Everyday Applications

Current Projects:

1. SPEDN auto-converts crypto to fiat for merchants, reducing rate of exchange rate risk while offering convenient customer payment options.
2. Slice offers real estate investing to anyone for as low as US$ 10,000 through fractional investment.

Near-future Projects:

1. CyClean plans to launch a blockchain-enabled electric vehicle (EV) fleet that mines crypto as users travel, thereby reducing emissions and rewarding users for doing so.
2. Digital construction platform Builderium connects contractors to clients around the world through blockchain, opening up a global marketplace for potential deals.

These are just a couple of the ways crypto currencies are breaking down barriers for people and corporations worldwide—allowing them to grow their personal wealth and enter the global markets.

Paying with Crypto Currency

If you are thinking about using crypto currency to make a payment, know the important differences between paying with crypto currency and paying by traditional methods. You do not have equivalent legal protection once you pay with crypto currency. Credit cards and debit cards have legal protections if something goes wrong.

For example, if you would like to dispute a sale, MasterCard features a process to assist you to get a refund. Crypto currency payments typically are not reversible. Once you pay with crypto currency, you simply cannot get a refund if the vendor sends it back. Before you purchase something with crypto currency, know a seller's reputation, where a vendor has to be found, and the way to contact someone if there is a drag.

Refunds Might Not Be in Crypto Currency

If refunds are offered, determine whether or not they are going to be in crypto currency, U.S. dollars, or something else. And how much will your refund be? The value of a crypto currency changes constantly. Before you purchase something with crypto currency, find out how the vendor calculates refunds.

Some information will likely be public. Although crypto currency transactions are anonymous, the transactions could also be posted to a public ledger, like Bitcoin's block chain. A block chain may be a public list of records that shows when someone transacts with crypto currency. Depending on the crypto currency, the information added to the block chain can include information like the transaction amount. The information can also include sender's and recipient's wallet addresses—a long string of numbers and letters linked to a digital wallet that stores crypto currency. Both the transaction amount and wallet addresses could be used to identify people using it.

Dangers Posed by Crypto Currency

Though crypto currency may not currently pose any systemic risk, its increasing popularity leading to price bubble, raises serious concerns for consumer and investor protection, and market integrity.

The crypto currency ecosystem may affect the existing payment and settlement systems which could, in turn, influence the transmission of monetary policy. Furthermore, being stored in digital/electronic media—electronic wallets—it is prone to hacking and operational risk, a few instances of which have already been observed globally. There is no established framework for recourse to customer problems and disputes resolution as payments by crypto currencies take place on a peer-to-peer basis without an authorised central agency which regulates such payments. There exists a high possibility of its usage for illicit activities, including tax avoidance.

The absence of information on counterparties in such peer-to-peer anonymous or pseudonymous systems could subject users to unintentional breaches of anti-money laundering laws as well as laws for combating the financing of terrorism. A globally coordinated approach is necessary to prevent abuses and to strictly limit interconnections with regulated financial institutions.

Remedial Measures

On a global level, regulatory responses to crypto currency have ranged from a complete *clamp down* in some jurisdictions to a comparatively *light touch regulatory approach*. The Securities and Exchange Commission (SEC) and the Commodity Futures Trading Commission (CFTC) have emerged as the primary regulators of crypto currencies in the United States, where these assets like most other jurisdictions, do not enjoy the legal tender status. Asian countries have experienced oversized concentration of crypto players. Thus, Japan and South Korea account for the biggest shares of crypto asset markets in the world. In the case of Bitcoins, half of transactions worldwide are carried out in Japan. In September 2017, Japan approved transactions by its exchanges in crypto currencies. China's exchanges hosted disproportionately large volumes of global Bitcoin trading until their ban recently.

In India, the Government and the Reserve Bank of India (RBI) are keeping a close watch on crypto currency and have issued pre-emptive cautionary warnings. In early April 2018, RBI barred its regulated entities from dealing in or providing services to any individual or business entities dealing with or settling in virtual currencies. Regulated entities which already provide such services were asked to exit the relationship within 3 months.

Developments on this front need to be monitored as some trading may shift from exchanges to peer-to-peer mode, which may also involve increased usage of cash. Possibilities exist as regards migration of crypto exchange houses to dark pools/cash and to offshore locations, thus raising concerns about money laundering as well as financing of terrorism.

Rapid changes in the landscape of payments industry, along with factors such as emergence of private digital tokens and the rising costs of managing fiat paper/metallic money, have led central banks around the world to explore the option of introducing fiat digital currencies. In India, an inter-departmental group has been constituted by the RBI to study and provide guidance on the desirability and feasibility to introduce a central bank digital currency.

In July 2018, RBI banned all banks, non-banking financial companies (NBFCs) and other financial institutions from dealing in crypto transactions.

Though crypto currency is not a legal tender yet, it is not illegal for Indians to buy, own or sell Bitcoins. Unlike regular currency, which has government backing, crypto currency can be held at one's own risk. In October 2018, crypto currency exchange Unocoin launched an ATM (or a kiosk) in Bengaluru for Indians to buy and sell Bitcoins. However, it was soon closed by the authorities for being illegal and without approval.

References

Ahmed, S. (2018), "Crypto Currency and Robots: How to Tax and Pay Tax on Them", S.C.L Rev, available at: https://papers.ssrn.com/sol3/papers.cfm?ab stract_id¼3083658.

Akins, B., Chapman, J. and Gordon, J. (2015), "A Whole New

World: Income Tax Considerations of the Bitcoin Economy", Pitt Tax Rev, available at: https:// papers.ssrn.com/sol3/papers.cfm?abstract_id¼2394738.

Bitcoin Mining Hardware Guide, available at: https://www.bitcoinmining.com/bit coin-mining-hardware.

Bitcoins in the US: White Listing and Licenses for a Clean Currency (German), available at: https://www.heise.de/newsticker/meldung/Bitcoins-in-denUSA-Whitelisting-und-Lizenzen-fuer-eine-saubere-Waehrung-2047456.html.

Brito, J., Shadab, H. and Castillo, A. (2014), "Bitcoin Financial Regulation: Securities, Derivatives, Prediction Markets, and Gambling", Colum Sci Technol L Rev, XVI, 144-219.

Bryans, D. (2014), "Bitcoin and Money Laundering: Mining for an Effective Solution", Ind L J, 89, 441-472.

Burge, M.E. (2016), "Apple Pay, Bitcoin, and Consumers: The ABCs of Future Public Payment Law", Hastings L J, 67, 1493-1549.

CoinMarketCap (2018), "Crypto Currency Market Capitalizations", available at: https://coin marketcap.com.

European Central Bank (2012), "Virtual Currency Schemes", Frankfurt: European Central Bank.

"General Terms and Conditions of Fidor Bank AG Regarding the Offer of the Exchange of Bitcoins on the Platform", (German), available at: https://www.bit coin.de/de/agbFidor.

Guadamuz, A. and Marsden, C. (2015), "Blockchains and Bitcoin: Regulatory Responses to Crypto Currencies", *First Monday*, available at: http://firstmonday.org/art icle/view/6198/5163.

Hacker, P. and Thomale, C. (2017), "Crypto-securities Regulation: ICOs, Token Sales and Crypto Currencies under EU Financial Law", Eur Co Financ L Rev, available at: https://papers.ssrn.com/sol3/papers.cfm?abstract_ id¼3075820.

Luther, W.R.B. (2016), "On What Grounds?", in Peirce, H. and Klutsey, B. (ed.), 'Reframing Financial Regulation: Enhancing Stability and Protecting Consumers', Arlington, VA: Mercatus Center at George Mason University, 391-415.

Maxwell, G. (2015), "Block Size Increase", available at:

https://lists.linuxfoundation.org/pipermail/bitcoin-dev/2015-May/007880.html.

Middlebrook, S. and Hughes S. (2014), "Regulating Crypto Currencies in the United States: Current Issues and Future Directions", Wm Mitchell L Rev, 40, 813-848.

Middlebrook. S and Hughes S. (2013), "Virtual Uncertainty: Developments in the Law of Electronic Payment and Financial Services", *Business Lawyer,* 69, 263-273.

Olson, C. (2016), "Money Laundering, Bitcoin and Blockchain: Anonymity, Transparency and Privacy are not Incompatible", available at:
https://www.finextra.com/blogposting/12663.

Ponsford, M. (2015), "A Comparative Analysis of Bitcoin and Other Decentralised Virtual Currencies: Legal Regulation in the People's Republic of China, Canada, and the United States", Hong Kong J Legal Stud, 9, 29-50.

Reyes, C. (2016), "Moving beyond Bitcoin to an Endogenous Theory of Decentralized Ledger Technology Regulation: An Initial Proposal", Vill L Rev, 61, 191-234.

"The Problem with Bitcoin that Everyone Seems to Ignore", available at:
https://www.eddit.com/r/Bitcoin/comments/374ss5/the_problem_with_bitcoin_that_ everyone_seems_to.

Tsukerman, M. (2015), "The Block is Hot: A Survey of the State of Bitcoin Regulation and Suggestions for the Future", Berkeley Technol L J, 30, 1128-1169.

Tu, K. and Meredith M. (2015), "Rethinking Virtual Currency Regulation in the Bitcoin Age", Wash L Rev, 90, 271-347.

"Why Bitcoin Fungibility is Essential", available at:
https://www.coindesk.com/bitcoinfungibility-essential.

6

Digital Finance and FinTech in India

Sumitha Franklin

Introduction

According to RBI Ombudsman Scheme for Digital Transactions, digital transaction means a payment transaction in a seamless system effected without the need for cash at least in one of the two legs, if not in both. This includes transactions made through digital/electronic modes wherein both the originator and the beneficiary use digital/electronic medium to send or receive money".

The Government of India has been taking numerous measures to develop and boost digital payments in the nation. As part of the 'Digital India' campaign, the government intends to create a 'digitally empowered' economy that is 'faceless, paperless, and cashless'. There are different types and modes of digital payments. Some of these include the use of debit/credit cards, mobile banking, mobile wallets, digital payment apps, unified payments interface (UPI) service, unstructured supplementary service data (USSD), bank prepaid cards, internet banking and so on.

Digital payment methods are often faster, easier, convenient and provide customers the flexibility to make payments from anywhere and at any time. These are decent options in contrast to traditional methods of payment and fasten up the transaction cycles. Post demonetization, people gradually began to embrace digital payments and even small merchants and retailers started accepting payments through the digital mode.

Current Status of Digital Transactions

Reserve Bank's Payment and Settlement Systems Vision,

2019-21 document is geared towards empowering every Indian with access to a bunch of e-payment options that are safe, secure, efficient, user friendly, quick and affordable. Further, the Department of Information Technology continued its initiatives to build a vigorous, strong and secured digital platform to assure smooth working of the payment and settlement systems in the country. The general objective is to strengthen digital payments across the country, both in terms of adoption and perception, and supported by customer-driven measures to increase the safety and security of the payment systems.

According to the RBI report, between financial years 2017 and 2019, the number of digital transactions in India shot up by 139 percent to 23,373 million. The value of these transactions jumped to ₹ 1,638,495 billion over the same period. It grew by 19.5 percent during 2018-19, compared to the growth of 22.2 percent during 2017-18. The Central Bank report says that, over the years, digital finance platform has witnessed unparalleled waves of innovation. It looks forward to raise the volumes of digital transactions by almost four times by 2021.

The share of digital transactions in the total volume of non-cash retail payments increased to 97.0 percent during 2019-20, up from 95.4 percent in the previous year. However, the extended period of lockdown arising on account of COVID-19 pandemic, resulted in restrained economic activities and lower discretionary payments, thereby leading to a fall in digital transactions.

COVID-19 pandemic has led to a reduction in digital transactions in India. The growth of currency with the people in India increased from 11.2 percent on February 28, 2020 to 14.5 percent on March 31, 2020, and further to 21.3 percent as on June 19, 2020 (12.8 percent a year ago). At the same time, the cumulative value of digital transactions during the period January-May 2020 declined by 25.5 percent as compared with a strong growth of 20.6 percent a year ago. Hence, digital retail transaction value growth decreased by 10.6 percent as compared to an increase of 31.3 percent last year. However, both these indicators recovered in the month of May 2020. Interestingly, transactions through immediate payment services (IMPS) started declining in February 2020 and the drop became sharper in April 2020. Unified payments interface (UPI) transaction volumes declined by 5.9 percent in March 2020 and further by 19.8 percent in April 2020, to slightly less than one billion transactions.

Apart from low demand during the lockdown, the deferment of operations by leading users of digital payments such as e-commerce and big techs, led to a decline in small value digital payments. The diminution in digital transactions during the lockdown period is indicative of the integration of the digital economy with the real economy. However, it gained momentum as the lockdown was gradually lifted and registered a record 1.34 billion transactions in June 2020.

COVID-19 and Lockdown

Since 2017, the financial services industry in India has seen visible growth and extensive adoption of modern mechanisms for digitization. Supplemented by proactive regulatory and policy efforts for financial inclusion and increased availability of reasonably priced internet and smart phones, digital finance payments and financial services carried via mobile phones and the internet have strengthened the economic system and changed the lives and economic prospects of individuals, organizations and governments across the developing world, consequently boosting the GDP and making the aim of financial inclusion a reality.

The waves of close halt of financial activities during the COVID-19 lockdown was felt across India—the prospering fintech industry been no exception. The best businesses and ideas arise during the most unpredictable and dubious occasions, and Indian start-ups have been quick to adjust to the speedily changing environment. In addition to core financial services offerings, digital fintech platforms have improved their delivery mechanisms to meet customer needs during this difficult time. For example, as demand for groceries and essential items has expanded, companies like PhonePe have enabled virtual stores on their mobile app to help local businesses to sell products online. Bangalore-based start-up Niki is leveraging voice chat in local vernacular languages including Tamil and Gujarati for its users to do digital transactions effortlessly.

The lockdown period has also observed a flood in online payments for certain kinds of products. What is coming is a significant shift in Indian consumer behaviour, as consumers develop new habits like instead of paying money at a local shop they use an app on their phone to order from the same store, which now can facilitate its operations on a mobile phone.

Simultaneously, the Government of India has ramped up its digital finance efforts as part of the COVID-19 economic response. It is vigorously promoting the use of real-time unified payments interface (UPI) for transactions. The Jan Dhan bank accounts, a key component of Prime Minister Modi's financial inclusion initiative over the past few years, has been especially beneficial during this pandemic time for direct cash transfers by the government to the most vulnerable sections of the society.

COVID-19 affected almost all business sectors, but some sectors had a positive impact, particularly the insurance sector. Businessmen and employers across India have realized the importance of insurance to keep themselves and their employees financially safe. Insurance penetration in India remains very low. These digital interventions are a welcome push forward for the industry and the consumers.

The post-COVID-19 period will see a shift in the Indian consumer behaviour including mounting preference for digital and contact less payments, renewed emphasis on savings and investments to handle uncertain issues and increased interest in health and life insurance to manage future unforeseen financial shocks. While this crisis has introduced ample challenges for

India's thousands of digital fintech businesses, many will emerge more resilient and primed for a global stage with Indian innovation leading the way.

As opposed to digital financial systems, physical channels are restrictive for even low-income populations. First, physical banking is relatively costlier and riskier for customers to perform even while engaging in basic financial activities like payments, savings, investments and remittances.

Second, it is very costly for firms, banks, insurance companies and other institutions to transact with them as it makes their operations infeasible and unsustainable. Digital channels offer a strong fix for the problems encountered by both consumers and financial institutions in traditional systems of finance.

Digital technologies have now become the most dominant tool for financial inclusion and are viewed as the smartest way to tap economic opportunity and quicken social development with economic empowerment. Digital tools have fostered speedier and more comprehensive development by drastically reducing financial service providers' costs and making services more convenient and accessible for users, especially low-income subscribers in remote locations.

Digital payments offer distinctive opportunities. Global trends indicate heightened customer expectations for value-added services, increased competition due to the emergence of FinTechs, new technologies, and an ever-changing administrative scene. These emerging global trends are expected to impact the Indian digital payments environment and give an impulse to the development of digital payments.

Towards FinTech

The term *FinTech* is a contraction of the words *finance* and *technology*. It refers to the technological start-ups that are emerging to challenge traditional banking and financial players and covers an array of services, from crowd funding platforms and mobile payment solutions to online portfolio management tools and international money transfers.

FinTech is an umbrella term coined in the recent past to denote technological innovation having a bearing on financial services. FinTech is a broad term that requires definition and currently, regulators are working on bringing out a common definition.

According to Financial Stability Board (FSB), of the Bank for International Settlements (BIS), "FinTech is technologically enabled financial innovation that could result in new business models, applications, processes, or products with an associated material effect on financial markets and institutions and the provision of financial services".

This definition aims at encompassing the wide variety of innovations in financial services enabled by technologies, regardless of the type, size and regulatory status of the innovative firm. The broadness of the FSB definition is useful in assessing and anticipating the rapid development of the financial system and financial institutions, and the associated risks and opportunities.

FinTech is broad term used to describe emerging technological innovations in the financial services sector, with ever increasing reliance on information technology. Starting as a term referring to the back-end technology used by large financial institutions, it has expanded to include technological innovation in the financial sector, including innovations in financial literacy and education, retail banking, investments etc.

Scope of FinTech: FinTech is a generic term coined in the recent past to denote technological innovation having a bearing on financial services. Financial services, including banking services, are at the threshold of a revolutionary change, driven by technological and digital innovations. A rapidly growing number of financial entities and technology firms are experimenting with technological and financial solutions which either modifies the way financial intermediation takes place or leads to disintermediation.

FinTech innovations have the potential to deliver a range

of benefits, in particular efficiency improvements and cost reductions. Technological developments are also fundamentally changing the way people access financial services and increasing financial inclusion.

Financial innovations (like derivatives) have become a focal point for a lot of attention, and some jurisdictions have decided to take a more active approach in facilitating this innovation. For this purpose, they have taken a variety of regulatory and supervisory initiatives such as regulatory sandboxes, innovation hubs, innovation incubators or accelerators, etc.

Technological start-ups are emerging to challenge traditional banking. Some of the major FinTech products and services currently used in the market place are peer-to-peer (P2P) lending platforms, crowd funding, block chain technology, distributed ledgers technology etc. These FinTech products are currently used in international finance, which bring together the lenders and borrowers, and seekers and providers of information, with or without a nodal intermediation agency.

FinTechs are becoming popular both with the users of banking services and investment funds, which see them as the future of financial sector. Even retail groups and telecom operators are looking for ways to offer financial services via their existing networks. This upsurge of activities raises questions over what kind of financial landscape will emerge in the wake of digital transformation.

Financial institutions and markets are seeking to increase their knowledge in relation to technological innovations, both through partnerships with tech companies and by investing in or acquiring such companies. Nonetheless, there are wide differences in the preparedness of market participants for these changes in practice.

Challenges

As far as digital payment system is concerned, managing fraud is the most challenging and tedious job. Handling fraud will require cooperation, and some degree of data sharing across the industry. One solution is to ensure that all fraud incidents, including transaction details are reported to the regulator. This data may be used to create a fraud registry. It is expected that the grievance redressal system will also serve as a mode for customers to report fraudulent transactions.

The RBI has been proactive and has given directions regards the security structure for banks and other monetary establishments. They have given rules to restrict risk of customers and made banks answerable for the security of client's funds. Safety and security in digital transactions are vital to acquire customer confidence.

Definitely, the shortage of cash has forced people, particularly in urban areas, to opt for digital payments like credit card, debit card, electronic funds transfer etc. But the real test will start when the cash crunch eases. It is to be ensured that people continue to use the e-payment methods.

Another important aspect is that post-demonetization, digital literacy is almost negligent. Training this set of people will be the next big challenge. Government should take a lead role in creating digital awareness among people.

Digital finance also has major technological and infrastructure challenges like inconsistent network coverage, lack of smart phone accessibility, less e-payment modes etc. A transition to the digital way of life has to take place gradually. Availability and quality of internet connection has to be maintained.

Poor internet facilities will lead to failure of transactions, which will discourage people from using digital payment methods. There is also an urgent need to invest in technology so that there are more e-payments modes.

Levying a surcharge on electronic transactions may also come as a setback. The costs associated with online payment through RTGS and NEFT modes have also created a hindrance. These methods are not only expensive, but also time-consuming. People should be offered incentives so that they are tempted to make a shift towards digital e-payments. Rewarding schemes and offers can increase the e-consumer base.

Digital inequality/digital divide in India is also a challenge for deeper penetration of digital payments. It refers to the gap between those able to benefit from the internet and those who are not. In India, we can see a wide disparity in knowledge and ability in using digital and information technology among individuals with different demographics and socio-economic backgrounds.

Conclusion

Moving towards a cashless economy is not an easy task in a country where cash is king. The government must take the lead to become cashless. There are challenges, but digital payment definitely has an undeniable future. As per the Credit Suisse report, India's digital payments are expected to reach US$ 1 trillion by 2023. More than 100 million people in India currently take recourse to digital payment mode at least once in a month in India. Banks and Fintech start-ups are also introducing several innovative digital payment modes each day. The days are not far away when India will be viewed as a 'Digital Economy'.

References

https://inc42.com/resources/digital-payments-in-india-current-challenges-and-growth-prospects.

https://m.rbi.org.in/Scripts/PublicationsView.aspx?id=19417.

https://rbidocs.rbi.org.in/rdocs/PublicationReport/Pdfs/CDDP03062019634B0EEF3F7144C3B65360B280E420AC.PDF.

https://www.credit-suisse.com/about-us/en/reports-research/global-wealth-rep.

https://www.outlookindia.com/outlookmoney/magazine/story/digital-payments-the-way-ahead-381.

https://www.rbi.org.in/scripts/AnnualReportPublications.aspx?Id=1293.

https://www.soleblogger.com/digital-payments-system-in-india.

Kumar, Rajesh, Mishra, Vagish and Saha, Somaraj Saha (2019), "Digital Financial Services in India: An Analysis of Trends in

Digital Payment", IJ RAR, May, Volume 6, Issue 2.

"Report of the High Level Committee on Deepening of Digital Payments", May 2019.

7

Direct Benefit Transfer (DBT) Initiative

Shiva Johri

To bring a paradigm shift in the delivery of services to the citizens, particularly the common man and the under-privileged sections of society of the country, the Government took a decision to start technology-driven DBT mechanism.

What is DBT?

Direct benefit transfer (DBT) is an initiative to reform the system of transfer subsidies initiated on January 1, 2013 by the Government of India. The goal of this programme is to pass subsidies to citizens into their bank accounts directly.

It aims at removing delays and leakages in crediting subsidies into bank accounts and attempts to change the pattern of transferring subsidies for various social welfare schemes like old age pension, scholarship, LPG subsidy, social security pensions etc. All relevant fund transferring accounts or processes are available on the website of the Central Plan Scheme Monitoring System (CPSMS), and is implemented by the Controller General of Accounts.

Rollout of DBT

Pursuant to the decision taken in the meeting of the National Committee on Direct Cash Transfers held by the Prime Minister, DBT was rolled out on January 1, 2013 in 43 districts for 26 select Centrally-sponsored schemes in a phased manner beginning with 20 districts on January 1, 2013, 11 districts from February 1, 2013 and the remaining 12 districts from March 1, 2013. Subsequently, the DBT rollout was further scaled up in a phased manner in other districts.

Phase II of the DBT was launched from July 1, 2013 in 78 identified districts. Three additional schemes were identified for DBT. The districts were identified on the basis of sufficient Aadhaar enrolment figures and financial inclusion. The schemes were selected on the basis of higher incidence of beneficiaries with bank accounts and where flow of funds was found to be relatively simpler. Accordingly, most schemes are related to scholarships, benefits to women and child labour.

Thus, benefits such as scholarships, pensions, and Mahatma Gandhi National Rural Employment Guarantee Scheme (MGNREGS) wages are directly credited to the bank or post office accounts of the identified beneficiaries.

DBT is designed to improve targeting, reducing corruption, eliminating waste, controlling expenditure, and facilitating reforms. Transfers that were taking place through paper and cash mode are now done through electronic transfers. This has been enabled by the rapid roll out of Aadhar (unique identity). DBT in tandem with such unique identification has ensured that the benefits reach the target groups faster and minimize inclusion and exclusion errors as well as corruption that are associated with the manual processes.

All public sector banks (PSBs) and regional rural banks (RRBs) have made provision so that the data collected by the Departments/Ministries/Implementing agencies concerned can be used for seeding the bank account details in the core banking system (CBS) of banks with Aadhaar. All PSBs have also joined the Aadhaar Payment Bridge of the National Payments Corporation of India (NPCI) for smooth transfer of benefits.

Prerequisites for Execution of DBT

These are as under:

1. Digitization of database of beneficiaries with Aadhaar number.
2. Opening of bank accounts of beneficiaries.
3. Enrolment of beneficiaries for generation of Aadhaar

numbers.

4. Digitized database to be seeded with Aadhaar number.
5. Bank accounts to be seeded with Aadhaar number.

Advantages of DBT

DBT provides the following advantages:

1. DBT aims to boost the Indian economy. Eventually, it will upgrade peoples' living style and enable them to lead a better life. DBT helps the society and especially the poor or people under low-income classes in India, for better sustainability, for them and their families.
2. People who receive DBT can solve the problem of intermediaries by purchasing goods at market prices. Thus, transparency in case of distributing funds including old age pension, scholarship funds, and social security pension funds could be attained.
3. Consolidated cash transfers to households which are getting benefits from multiple sources and in multiple forms.
4. Improved efficiency of social safety net, consolidated income support programme for the poor and elimination of multiple sources of subsidy.
5. Positive institutional externalities.
6. Freeing of administrative system from exercise of control and focussing on development.
7. Maximizing benefits from expenditure on welfare schemes which leads to overall human development.

DBT is primarily meant for the under-privileged and weaker sections of the society. DBT has been launched in North-Eastern States and is operational in Tripura and Sikkim as well. Various welfare schemes for scheduled castes (SCs), scheduled tribes (STs), other backward classes (OBCs), women, children, senior citizens and disabled have been included in the DBT mechanism.

Types of DBT Transfer

DBT comprises all welfare and subsidy schemes

administered directly or by the implementing agencies, which include cash/assistance transfers to individuals, from all Ministries/Departments of Government of India. Cash transfer to the actual beneficiary involves agreements or programme elements under which cash rewards are distributed to individual beneficiaries through the government.

In-kind transition from the government to individual recipients involves schemes or elements of schemes in which the government delivers benefits to individuals. Besides these two classes of schemes, there is another group of transfers from the government to various non-government officials who help in facilitating various schemes for the government till the last mile. This group involves allocation of money in the form of honorariums, bonuses, etc. to different officials in government structures such as community employees, NGOs.

Limitations of DBT

These can be listed as follows:

1. Value of transfers may be inadequate, especially if they are not indexed to market price and inflation.
2. Access to banks/ATMs and markets may vary across locations.
3. Recipients may use cash for non-specified purposes, thereby negating the purpose of subsidy.

Conclusion

There is scope for further research on DBT. Researchers may work on the security area to stop fraudulent practices in the area of DBT to ensure transparency. Furthermore, finding new schemes to address different class of needy people could be another focus area with due relevance to DBT. Focus should also be made for mobile connectivity for transfers under DBT. This easy transfer system would facilitate transfer of funds, and also enhance digitalization of the system. Measures for implementing DBT effectively in States could be suggested by studying the fluctuations after its initiation. The aim of the government is to enable complete Aadhar-based DBT system for all kinds of welfare schemes in India.

DBT has ensured an updated lifestyle for the Indian people. The main goal of the DBT is to ensure "life worth living" for the residents of India. For ensuring a better plan, the Government of India has taken further steps for a better-sustained technology of DBT. The government should be more conscious about the fraud prevalence in the DBT system, if any.

To sum up, DBT has emerged as an important mechanism for transfers to citizens under different welfare/subsidy schemes of the government and in future its scope is likely to enlarge substantially. DBT has helped in efficient processing of the transfers and weeding out ghost beneficiaries.

References

Chakrabarti, R. (2014), "Show Me the Cash: Direct Cash Transfer in India", available at: https://papers.ssrn.com/sol3/papers.418https://dbtbharat.gov.in.

Joseph, L., Lekha, T., Boban, D., Jose, P. and Jeemon, P. (2019), "Perceived Facilitators and Barriers of Enrolment, Participation, and Adherence to a Family-based Structured Lifestyle Modification Interventions in Kerala, India: A Qualitative Study".

Joy, J. (2018), "A Critical Analysis of Direct Benefit Transfer in India", *Indian Journal of Economics and Development*, 6(8), pp. 1-7.

Kasane, R.A. (2015), "A Study of Direct Benefit Transfer with Special Reference to MGNREGA", *The Business and Management Review, 5*(4), p. 38.

Mithra, S.A., Kar, M.K., Mohapatra, T., Robin, S., Sarla, N., Seshashayee, M., Singh, K., Singh, A.K., Singh, N.K. and Sharma, R.P. (2016), "DBT Propelled National Effort in Creating a Mutant Resource for Functional Genomics in Rice", *Current Science*, pp. 543-548, available at: https://www.jstor.org/stable/24907913?seq=1#metadata_info_tab_contents..

Roy, T.N. (2019), "Direct Benefit Transfer (DBT) of Fertilizer Subsidy in India: Issues and Related Aspects", *International*

Journal of Bio-resource and Stress Management, 10(3), pp. 329-334.

Selvam, V. and Velmurugan, G. (2015), "An Empirical Study on DBT Awareness", *Mediterranean Journal of Social Sciences*, 6(5), p. 229.

8

Digital Financial Services and Mobile Banking

Mazhar Mohammad

Introduction

Income inequalities are widening despite rapid progress made by several countries across the globe. Most of the people in developing world do not have formal access to banking channels due to varied reasons either economic or geographical. Penetration of financial services in poor countries like Africa and Sub-Saharan Africa are believed to be very low and hence they can be fertile grounds to study and assess the impact of digitalization of financial services in alleviating poverty.

While India cannot be considered a poor country with US$ 3 trillion of GDP and US$ 2,169 of per capita GDP, which is 17 percent of world's average per capita GDP (World Bank, 2019), however, the fact remains that many Indians are poor and even today it is estimated that millions of people are struggling with poverty despite the country having the tag of being one of the fastest growing economies in the world. One of the main reasons for this dire situation is lack of access to credit and savings.

Vision for Financial Inclusion

RBI Committee on Medium Term Path to Financial Inclusion, Chaired by Deepak Mohanty in 2015, has set the vision for financial inclusion as, "convenient access to a basket of basic formal financial products and services that should include savings, remittances, credit, government-supported insurance and pension products to small and marginal farmers and low income households at reasonable cost with adequate protection, progressively supplemented by social cash transfers, besides increasing access of small and marginal enterprises to formal finance with a greater reliance on technology to cut costs and improve service delivery...".

Among the poor countries, Kenya seems to have set the example as it took the lead way back in 2007 to digitalize its financial services through its telecom operator Safaricom. This company rolled out M-Pesa, a mobile banking service which revolutionized its financial services space. In 2006, it was estimated that only 26.7 percent of Kenyan adult population was having access to formal financial services and this figure jumped to 75.3 percent (FinAccess, 2016). In his seminal work, Stanford Economist Pascaline Dupas found that eliminating account and opening costs also played a significant role in dramatic jump in savings accounts and investments among market vendors (Dupas and Robinson, 2013).

Eventually, Kenya topped the list of 21 nations in Brookings Financial and Digital Inclusion Project, 2015 rankings. These rankings were declared on the basis of 33 parameters, covering four dimensions of financial inclusion, viz. country commitment, mobile capacity, regulatory environment and adoption (Villasenor et al., 2015). In another study by Silvia Prinait, it was found that offering a free account to a female family head in Nepal led to a rise in deposits. Households responded better to health shocks, spent 20 percent more on education and consumption of meat and fish increased by 15 percent. It was also found that more than 80 percent retained their account and continued to use it even after a period of 12 months (Prina, 2015). Lasse Brune and others studied the impact of savings on rural farmers of Malawi. Their study concluded that farmers with access to savings account enhanced cultivated land by 7 percent, their crop output increased by 15 percent and expenditure by 10 percent. Their savings also jumped throughout the harvest season (Brune et al., 2015).

Digital Payments Revolution

Financial Services are at the cusp of a revolutionary change, driven by technological and digital innovations. Added to this, the increasing penetration of internet and advent of smart phones has facilitated wider usage of mobile banking, which has become almost ubiquitous, and appears to have sharply accelerated the process of digitalizing financial services.

Table 8.1: Milestones in Digital Payment Infrastructure in India

Period	Technology Introduced
1980s-1990s	• Introduction of electronic clearing services and electronic funds transfer. • Debit and credit cards issued by banks.
2000-2005	• New Secure Fund settlement systems introduced. • Real Time Gross Settlement (RTGS). National Electronic Funds Transfer (NEFT).
2006-2010	• Payments and Settlement Systems Act • Launch of Aadhar, a unique biometric identification program with the aim of providing a Unique ID to every Indian citizen. • Launch of IMPS (Immediate Payment Services).
2011-2014	• Launch of Rupay card payment scheme • Implementation of NACH (National Automated Clearing House). • Introduction of Aadhar Enabled Payment Systems.
2015-2018	• Transactions relating to IMPS and PPI (prepaid instruments). • Bharat QR introduced, Bharat Interface for Money (BHIM) mobile app launched.

Source: KPMG Report on Mobile Banking, 2019.

According to GSMA, which represents the interest of 750 mobile operators and 450 companies around the world with 290 live services in 95 countries and 372 million active accounts, mobile money is entering the mainstream and becoming the path to financial inclusion in most low income countries. As per its latest, 'State of the Industry Report on Mobile Money, 2019':

1. One billion registered accounts for mobile money services.
2. Value of daily transactions carried through mobile money is US$ 2 billion.
3. 77 mobile money deployments have more than one million 90 day active accounts.
4. In 2019, for the first time, a majority of digital transactions were carried out through mobile money. The ratio of digital to cash based transactions has nearly increased by 50 percent since 2017.
5. According to its survey, 60 percent of mobile money service providers partnered with humanitarian organizations to deliver mobile money enabled cash vouchers to over 2.7 unique mobile money accounts with the objective of pushing financial services amongst the poor and marginalized sections of the society.

Mobile Banking

Mobile phones, as a medium for providing banking services, have been attaining increased importance. Reserve Bank of India (RBI) brought out a set of operating guidelines on mobile banking for banks in October 2008, according to which only banks which are licensed and supervised in India and have a physical presence in India are permitted to offer mobile banking after obtaining necessary permission from the RBI. The guidelines focus on systems for security and inter-bank transfer arrangements through RBI's authorized systems. On the technology front, the objective is to enable development of inter-operable standards so as to facilitate funds transfer from one account to any other account in the same or any other bank on a real time basis irrespective of the mobile network a customer has subscribed to.

Mobile Banking and Financial Inclusion: Developments in mobile telephony, as also the mobile phone density in the

India, present a unique opportunity to leverage the mobile platform to meet the objectives and challenges of financial inclusion. By harnessing the potential of mobile technology, large sections of the unbanked and under-banked society can be empowered to become inclusive through the use of electronic banking services.

The Payment and Settlement Systems (PSS) Act, 2007, empowers the Reserve Bank of India to authorize and regulate entities operating payment systems in the country. RBI has, over a period of time, placed importance on the move towards electronic payments and thereby a *less-cash* society. Towards this end, the RBI has been promoting and nurturing the growth of various modes of electronic payments including the pre-paid payment instruments, card payments, mobile banking etc.

The Payment Systems Vision Document, 2012-15 of the RBI, reflected the commitment towards provision of safe, efficient, accessible, inclusive, interoperable and authorised payment and settlement systems in the country. Recent experience shows that the share of paper-based instruments in the volume of total non-cash transactions has been declining in favour of electronic payments. Though overall volume of transactions in mobile banking is low, there has been a significant growth in the volumes recently.

Mobile Banking: Regulatory Framework: Recognising the potential of mobile as a channel for offering financial services in the country, RBI issued the first set of guidelines on mobile banking in October 2008. The mandate was that all transactions should originate from one bank account and terminate in another bank account. At that time, a few banks had already started offering information-based services like balance enquiry, stop payment instruction of cheques, transactions enquiry, location of the nearest ATM/branch etc. through this medium.

The guidelines issued by the RBI in October 2008, permitted banks to facilitate funds transfer from one bank account to another bank account, both for personal remittances and for purchase of goods and services. Banks were directed on the regulatory/supervisory issues, registration of customers for mobile banking, to ensure technology standards, interoperability, inter-bank clearing and settlement arrangements for fund transfers, customer grievance and redressal mechanism and transaction limits in an attempt to ensure safe and secure transfer of funds. Under extant regulatory prescriptions, there is no monetary restriction on funds transfer effected through mobile banking as it is left to the risk perception of each bank and policies approved by their respective boards.

In line with these guidelines, banks have been offering mobile banking services to their customers through various channels such as SMS, USSD channel, mobile banking application etc. However, real time inter-bank mobile banking payments have been facilitated through the setting up of the inter-bank mobile payment services, now termed as immediate payment services (IMPS), and operated by the National Payments Corporation of India (NPCI) with the approval of the RBI. The IMPS has enhanced the efficiency of mobile banking by enabling real time transfer of funds between bank accounts and providing a centralised inter-bank settlement service for mobile banking transactions.

Various Channels for Mobile Banking

Mobile Banking: SMS-based Channel: SMS is a popular and widely used channel in mobile phones. It is ubiquitously available in all handsets irrespective of make and model and also GSM and CDMA enabled handsets. Most customers are very conversant with the SMS channel and use the same for various services including the short messaging. Many popular mobile VAS services such as cricket, jokes, horoscopes, etc. are based on SMS and widely used by the customers.

Given the advantages offered by SMS channel, many banks have offered mobile banking services through the SMS channel. This includes non-financial services such as balance enquiry, mini statement, cheque book request, transaction alerts etc., and financial services such as funds transfer, mobile/DTH recharge, bill payments etc.

Mobile Banking: USSD-based Channel: Unstructured supplementary service data (USSD) is a protocol used by GSM cellular telephones to communicate with the telecom service provider's systems. USSD can be used for WAP browsing, pre-paid call-back service, mobile-money services, location-based content services, menu-based information services, and as part of configuring the phone on the network.

USSD messages are up to 182 alphanumeric characters in length. Unlike short message service (SMS) messages, USSD messages create a real-time connection during a USSD session. The connection remains open, allowing a two-way exchange of a sequence of data. This makes USSD more interactive and advantageous than services that use SMS.

USSD platform which is MNO dependent can be efficiently used by the mobile banking platforms. Realizing the benefits and potential of USSD-based mobile banking, some of the banks have launched USSD-based mobile banking services, e.g. State Bank of India, Canara Bank, ICICI Bank, with the help of telecom aggregators who in turn have tied up with few MNOs. For instance, ICICI Bank has tied up with Idea, Aircel, Reliance and MTNL for offering USSD platform to its customers on their GSM network.

Mobile Banking: Application-based: All banks who have received the approval from RBI for mobile banking are offering the application-based mobile banking channel to their customers. Customers can download the mobile banking application and perform variety of services including the following: (a) non-financial transactions such as balance enquiry, mini statement, cheque book request, and (b) financial transactions such as funds transfer, mobile/DTH recharge, bill payments etc.

The mobile application is offered on various platforms such as Java, Symbian, Blackberry OS, Windows, Android, Apple iOS etc. Many banks have made the mobile application available in app stores such as Google, Apple, Blackberry, etc. for easy search and download by the customers.

Following are the advantages of application-based mobile banking:

1. Applications once downloaded are easy to use for the customers who are proficient in using the smart phone based applications.
2. Banks have made these applications compliant with most of the latest operating systems covering a large range of smart phones in use.
3. It has been experienced by the banks that once customer has used the application-based mobile banking, he continues to use the same unless there is a change of handset and/or mobile number.
4. The application-based mobile banking can also communicate using SMS and GPRS (data) channels with mobile banking system of the bank.

RBI's Technical Committee on Mobile Banking

Reserve Bank of India constituted a Technical Committee (Chairman: B. Sambamurthy), to study in depth, the present challenges faced in mobile banking, the adoption of particular technologies to meet the requirements of banks as well as vast numbers of mobile users and draw up a roadmap for implementation of the solutions. [1]

Major recommendations of the Committee which submitted its report in 2014 were as under:

1. Banks need to explore other means of facilitating customer/user registration process for mobile banking which does not require a visit to the bank branch. The potential of inter-operable ATM networks and business correspondent arrangements has to be effectively harnessed towards meeting this objective. Standardization is required in: (a) user registration for mobile banking, (b) user authentication process and (c) user interfaces. Recognising the crucial role that customer/user awareness

plays in adoption of any technology for financial transactions, as well as the need for optimal utilization of resources, the joint customer education programmes by banks will go a long way in facilitating usage of mobile banking.

2. Mobile network operators (MNOs) need to see a business model in it for themselves and play out their role in ensuring that mobile banking reaches its full potential by co-operating with banks in their endeavour to provide the appropriate technology/channel to the targeted users. Mobile banking can result in customer stickiness and reduce churn for MNOs. Mobile banking can increase revenue to MNOs and reduce costs to banks. The current solutions already provided by banks and various technological alternatives available can be put in place through a concerted effort between banks and telecom service providers.
3. Common mobile banking applications and common technological platforms need to be built for reaping the benefits of *network effects*. While bank-specific applications and individual platforms have a major role in building brand loyalty, an alternate uniform/common platform, interoperability and similar seamless transactional experience to the users/customers of all banks would encourage mobile banking.

The Government of India can explore the options of offering fiscal incentives/economic subventions to the stakeholders in order to ensure participation of various players to offer the solutions recommended here in this Report. The Committee would like to draw attention to similar law *Lei Do Bem* (Law of the Goods) enacted by Brazil in October 2013 which mandates that smart phones give visibility to Brazilian made apps by either pre-loading phones with these home-grown apps or providing a dedicated market place on smart phones to display them.

Impact of FinTech Evolution on Indian Financial Services

Financial innovation backed by technology rapidly transformed itself into a young and vibrant sector which is widely recognized as FinTech. Several tech driven start-ups populate into this sector increasing the heat on traditional bankers and non-banking finance companies to embrace the change. Report by NASSCOM estimates around 400 FinTech companies operating in India at various stages. Soon FinTech also looked like a potential solution for the problems faced by traditional financial institutions like low penetration, lack of credit history of borrowers and excessive cash transactions in the economy.

Despite introducing PMJDY program in 2016, India still has the second largest unbanked population of 191 million in the world (Global Findex, 2017) and 48 percent of the accounts opened under this scheme are believed to be inactive with no withdrawals for a period of one year (World Bank 2018). This is providing a huge opportunity for FinTech players to identify, innovate and provide the service which suits them best. According to RBI Working Group 2017 Report, FinTech industry grew by 282 percent between 2013 and 2014 and valued at US$ 450 million in 2015. In a recent report by Research and Markets, Indian FinTech Industry is valued at ₹ 1920.16 billion in 2019 and expected to reach ₹ 6,207.41 billion by 2025 which is a compounded annual growth rate of 22.7 percent between 2020 and 2025. This report also notes that India has a FinTech adoption rate of 87 percent among the emerging markets in the world against the world average adoption rate of 64 percent.

FinTech and Financial Inclusion in India: Developing inclusive financial systems is an important component for economic and social progress as empirical evidence shows that countries with deeper financial inclusion tend to grow faster and reduce income inequality (Beck et al., 2007). Government of India is proactively pushing for financial inclusion with the main objective of bringing marginalized sections of the society into main banking channels by effectively making use of FinTech solutions. In this regard it initiated following steps.

Pradhan Mantri Jan-Dhan Yojana (PMJDY)

PMJDY can be considered as a flagship program which aims at offering savings deposit account, with remittance, credit, insurance and pension in an affordable manner. Government of India is so committed that it opened around 1.5 crore accounts on the very first day and went on to create Guinness World Record. Their certificate says, "the most bank accounts opened in 1 week as a part of financial inclusion campaign is 18,096,130 and was achieved by the Department of Financial Services, Government of India from 23-29 August 2014". PMJDY program appears to have been an instant hit as adults owning savings accounts jumped to 80 percent (Global Findex, 2017). This figure stood at 53 percent in 2014, before the commencement of PMJDY, against a global average of 62 percent (Demirguc-Kunt Asli et al., 2015). This bank account is further linked with mobile and Aadhar number to deliver direct benefit of subsidies to the poor through biometric authentication. This became popular as 'JAM' trinity in which 'J' stands for Jan-Dhan accounts, 'A' for Aadhar (the 12 digit unique identification number) and 'M' for mobile number of the account holder. Undoubtedly, it has succeeded in plugging the leakages in government subsidies.

Payments Banks

In furtherance of the objective of financial inclusion, RBI issued payment bank licenses to 11 entities out of 41 applicants. Bharti Airtel launched India's first payment bank called Airtel Payments Bank in March 2017. That was soon followed by opening up of India Post Payment Bank, Paytm Payment Bank, and Fino Payment Bank and. These payment banks have two main objectives:

1. To mobilize small savings among the marginalized sections.

2. To act as a money transfer intermediaries for migrant labour, small businesses, low-income households, and others in the unorganized sector.

However, payment bank license come with a restriction that they cannot lend money but have to deploy the savings, which they mobilize, in government securities and bank deposits. Despite some prominent names from Indian corporate sector bagging the license, a few of them like Cholamandalam Distribution Services, Sun Pharmaceuticals and Tech Mahindra, surrendered their licenses within 6 months citing long gestation on road to profitability whereas Aditya Birla Idea Payment Bank, surrendered its license in October 2019. This has raised doubts about the commercial viability of these entities. However, Raghuram Rajan, the then RBI Governor remarked that it reflects companies failure to properly assess the businesses potentiality while applying for the license.

Small Finance Banks

To make deep inroads into unbanked areas, Government of India along with the RBI permitted establishment of small finance banks (SFBs). RBI guidelines in this regards clearly point out that such banks shall focus on underserved regions of North-East, East and Central regions of India and should target marginalized segments of small businesses and entities in the unorganized sector, poor households, and farmers through credit and savings products. Minimum 25 percent of SFBs shall be located in unbanked areas of villages where the population is less than 9,999. As these entities are new kids on the block and having received licenses in September 2015, their real impact is yet to be felt but they have a lot of potentiality and growth opportunities.

According to Micrometer (MFIN, 2018) report, low income states (LIS) and North-Eastern States (NES) collectively have a total of 85.7 million low income households with a potential credit demand of ₹ 18.3 trillion and possible saving potentiality of ₹ 21.4 trillion. Moreover, it is estimated that micro and small enterprises from these regions have a debt demand of ₹ 21.8 trillion and savings potentiality of ₹ 5.9 trillion. SFBs are expected to constructively exploit these opportunities by making use of high technology to scale up their activities with low operational costs.

Self-help Groups-Bank Linkage Program (SHG-BLP)

SHG is an informal financial network of 15-20 people playing a critical role at grass root levels in promotion of financial inclusion. These networks pool funds and sanction loans to members on need basis. This group will eventually form a link with the bank to establish a formal relationship so that SHG as an entity can make deposits and borrow money from the bank. This model which started as a pilot project by NABARD way back in 1992-93 by linking 500 SHGs to the formal financial institutions ultimately became the largest micro finance program in the world in terms of client base and outreach. SHG-BLP finally evolved as a cost effective mechanism for the unbanked poor households.

As per Micro Finance in India, 2019-20 report, released by NABARD, SHG-BLP program touched 12.4 crore households with 102 lakh SHGs which mobilized over ₹ 26,000 crore of deposits and sanctioned annual loan of ₹ 77,000 crore. SHGs outstanding credit as on March 31, 2020 stood at ₹1,08,000 crore. In 2015, it launched the e-Shakti project for digitizing all SHGs. The project is currently being implemented in 254 districts across the country and as on March 31, 2020, 6.54 lakh SHGs involving 72 lakh members in more than 98,000 villages have been on-board at the e-Shakti portal. 'e-Shakti' portal captures the financial and non-financial profiles of SHGs and their members and provides up-to-date data to bankers and their stakeholders at a click of button (State of Micro Finance India Report, 2020).

Social Security Measures through Insurance

Albeit, Government of India introduced life and accident

risk insurance through schemes like Pradhan Mantri Suraksha Bima Yojana, Pradhan Mantri Jeevan Jyothi Yojana and Atal Pension Yojana etc. as a part of financial inclusion for the benefit of the marginalized sections, the insurance sector as such in India is yet to harness the complete benefits of FinTech revolution.

Life insurance policies even today cannot be bought and sold online while some progress in this regard has been made in the general insurance space. Apart from the above steps, Government of India along with RBI is trying to build a FinTec eco-system to actively push for financial inclusion by leveraging on technology. The FinTech companies across the nation are taking advantage of these initiatives by expanding their services.

Conclusion

India is not only a poor country but also, many lack basic education. Hence, the first step in successful implementation of programs related to financial inclusion requires the spread of financial literacy. In this regard, even civil society, apart from main stakeholders like banks and financial institutions, should actively take part.

As empirical evidence from around the world, and including India, hints that technology can accelerate the path of financial inclusion by quickly reaching the needy and cutting the geographical barriers. Government should invest in digitalizing financial inclusion programs as they are found not only to be effective but also less corrupt while delivering to the target audience. Government should play a key role in building digital infrastructure and FinTech eco-system and these services should be provided at an affordable cost.

There should be customer centric approach and 'One Method Fits All' kind of approach should be avoided while designing the products, to suit the needs of poor customers. Moreover, there should be time bound and proper grievance redressal mechanism to effectively address the problems faced by the consumers. Also, any discussion on financial inclusion would be incomplete unless there is an objective and scientific assessment of progress made in this area. There is a need to go beyond the data points collected from financial institutions alone and genuine feedback should be obtained from the beneficiaries as well.

References

Central Bank of Kenya (2016), "FinAccess Household Survey", February.

"Digital Finance for All: Powering Inclusive Growth in Emerging Economies", McKinsey Global Institute, September 2016.

Dupas, Pascaline and Robinson, Jonathan (2013), "Savings Constraints and Micro enterprise Development: Evidence from a Field Experiment in Kenya", *American Economic Journal: Applied Economics,* 5(1): 163-192.

Gwer, F., Odero, J. and Totolo, E. (2019), "Digital Credit Audit Report: Evaluating the Conduct and Practice of Digital Lending in Kenya", FSD Kenya.

KPMG India (2019), "FinTech in India: Powering Mobile Payments", August.

KPMG India and NASSCOM (2016), "FinTech in India: A Global Growth Story", June.

"High Level Committee on Deepening of Digital Payments", Chairman Nandan Nilekani, May 2019.

Lewis, Robin J., Villasenor, John and West, Darell M. (2015), "Five Key Findings from the 2015 Financial and Digital Inclusion Project Report and Scorecard".

National Bank for Agriculture and Rural Development (NABARD) (2019), "Status of Micro Finance in India: 2019 -20", Mumbai.

Reserve Bank of India (2020), "National Strategy on Financial Inclusion, 2019-2024' Mumbai, January 11.

Reserve Bank of India (2019), "Payments and Settlement Systems in India: Vision 2019-21", Mumbai, May 15.

Reserve Bank of India (2017), "Working Group on FinTech and Digital Banking", Mumbai, November.

"Research and Impact of Digital Financial Services", Working Paper 22633, National Bureau of Economic Research, September 2016.

Silvia, Prina (2015), "Banking the Poor via Savings Accounts", *Journal of Development Economics*, 115: 16-31.

"State of the Industry Report on Mobile Money, 2019", GSM

Association.
"The Global Findex Database, 2017: Measuring Financial Inclusion and FinTech Revolution".

9

Digital Divide and Education in India

Bishweshwar Bhattacharjee and
Bireshwar Bhattacharjee

Introduction

Despite the sharp rise in telecommunication access in the developing nations, the global digital divide is getting wider [1]. The education system across the globe has undergone major transformation with the exceptionally fast paced change in technological domain of knowledge. As a result, ICT in its own way has managed to make a permanent place for itself in the education sector—specifically in school education in the Indian context [2]. In a developing country like India, advances in ICTs have brought in a lot of opportunities and perhaps a whole lot of challenges as well. One of the main challenges is the considerable gap between the information have-s and information have-nots—what we call the digital divide. And, this digital gap starts right from the school [3].

Our schools—primarily government schools—are ill-equipped in terms of infrastructure and basic facilities. Our teachers are not adequately trained to infuse ICT in education, and execution of many enthusiastic policies are done half-heartedly, thus, leaving the less privileged segment of children, who come from the lower socio-economic class of society and are largely dependent on government school system for their education, with very little or no access to digital learning [2]. This frustrating situation creates a "digital divide", which refers to the gap between people with effective access to digital and information technology and those with very limited or no access at all. It includes the imbalances in physical access to technology as well as the imbalances in resources and skills needed to effectively participate as a digital citizen. This paper attempts to look into the status of education and digital penetration in India, based on NSS Survey, an attempt first of its kind as far as known.

Digital Divide

Digital divide, arguably the most intriguing phrase of the present day seems to have had its origin in the United States. Many consider Andy Grove as one of the creators of digital divide network. Few others say the credit goes to Larry Irvin. According to Benton Foundation, former President Bill Clinton first used the term during the discussion on National Information Infrastructure, in 1993. Though there are controversies existing as to who coined the term, there is a wider acceptance on the increasing gap between information have-s and information have-nots. A report of the UN that appeared in New York Times, lamented the growing digital divide in developing countries. The Indian subcontinent is struggling to stay alive with the growing digital divide, leaving the poor illiterates poorer and the rich people richer [3].

Digital Divide in Education

Schools across the country have been closed for a good amount of period due to COVID-19 pandemic. However, this holds different connotation for different people. For a child in urban Himachal Pradesh, where internet penetration is higher than 70 percent, it likely means online schooling, zoom classes and digital textbooks. For a child in rural Odisha, where less than 6 percent of households have internet facilities, such options are out of the question. The national capital has the highest internet access, and Himachal Pradesh and Kerala are the only other States where more than half of all households have internet. At the other end of the spectrum is Odisha, where only one in ten homes have internet. There are ten other States with less than 20 percent internet penetration, including states such as Karnataka and Tamil Nadu, also known as software hubs [4].

Review of Literature

Thakur [3] observed that even though computer education was introduced twenty to twenty-five years back in some urban schools in the country, most schools in rural and sub-urban India, especially government schools still do not have adequate teachers, let alone a computer laboratory. There is a growing discrepancy between those who have access to information and those who do not.

The second group comprises of the majority and most of them live in rural areas of developing countries. There is a gap among those who are able to take advantage of new ICT opportunities and those who are not. Hence, digital divide affects many nations of the developing world (Bera) [5]; Bansode and Patil [6]).

Singh [7] viewed that in India, all people do not have access to internet and ICT, and an amazingly large number of people especially from the rural areas do not have the abilities to use ICT in a proper way and, therefore cannot draw the advantages from its usage. The issues of digital divide are posing a Herculean task before the Government of India to provide maximum benefits to the stakeholders. The paper also revealed that the problems of digital divide also exist within and among various States of India.

While some people are rich and have many resources, others do not. The educational system of India also has been slow to achieve the set target framed by various commissions and committees and schemes launched from time to time. The lack of sound ICT strategies and policies in India is the main cause behind these.

Panda et al. [8] observed that the phenomenon of digital discrimination prevailing among various social, political and working groups has led to the emergence of digital information rich and digital information poor groups within societies and perhaps in the global environment. Libraries have long been essential agents in fostering peace and human values. Libraries are now operating digitally, and their digital services open up a new channel to the universe of knowledge and information, connecting cultures across geographical and social boundaries. Similar conclusions were reflected in studies by Kaur and Singh [9], Mohanti [10], Bridges [11], Chopra [12], Cullen [13], Kumar [14] etc.

Objectives and Methodology of the Study

The present study frames the objective of status of education and digital penetration across various regions of India.

The data was collected from the NSS 75th round on 'Key Indicators of Household Social Consumption on Education in India'. The statistical tools of average were used for the analysis. Sub-divided and multiple bar diagrams have been used for graphical illustration.

Digital Penetration in India

The level of digital penetration is gauged firstly from the household level digital penetration rates, both for rural and urban areas. The level of digital penetration on all-India basis for rural areas is quite low (19 percent). In North India, the level of digital penetration is the highest (18.9 percent) followed by South India (14.6 percent) and is the lowest in Eastern India (Figure 9.1).

The level of digital penetration on all-India basis for urban areas is relatively high (65 percent). In North India, the level of digital penetration is the highest (27.6 percent) followed by South India (23.5 percent) and is the lowest in Central India (Figure 9.2).

An additional detailed analysis was undertaken for gauging the level of digital penetration at the individual level, by gender positions. As far as the ability to operate computer is concerned, both males and females had greater ability in Southern India and it was found the lowest in Eastern India.

Nonetheless, the gap is more in Central India and less in Southern India.

Figure 9.1: Level of Digital Penetration in Rural Areas at the Household Level

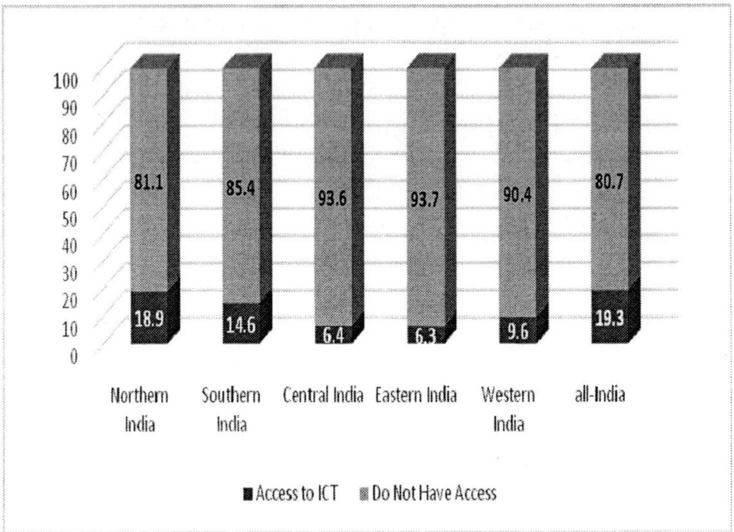

Source: Authors' calculations based on NSS 75th round data on 'Key Indicators of Household Social Consumption on Education in India'.

Whereas, regards the ability to operate internet is concerned, both males and females possessed greater ability in Southern India and it was found to be the lowest in Eastern India. Also, both males and females had more ability in Northern India. In case of overall disparity in gender, it was more in parts of Central India, followed by Eastern India and Southern India.

Education and Digital Divide in India

In this section, we will look at the levels of education and digital divide across regions, both in rural and urban India and also try to figure out the rural-urban gap in this regard (Table 9.1).

At all-India level, the level of education and internet usability was low as far as rural areas were concerned. The percentage of educated persons was merely 30 percent.

More surprisingly, the internet accessibility was merely 13 percent, while only 11 percent used internet. In Northern India, whereas, nearly 40 percent people were educated, 21 percent had internet accessibility and merely 19 percent used it.

Figure 9.2: Level of Digital Penetration in Urban Areas at the Household Level

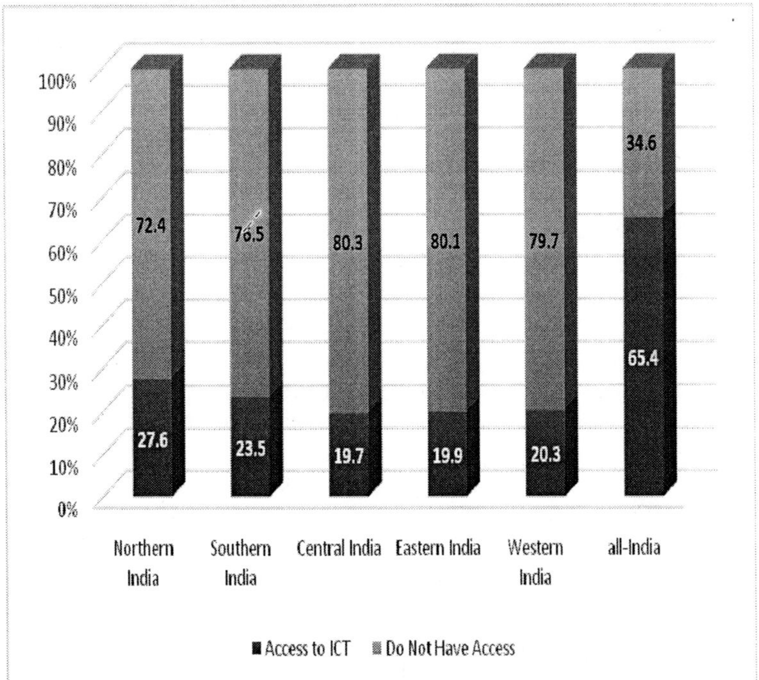

Source: Authors' calculation based on NSS 75th round data on 'Key Indicators of Household Social Consumption on Education in India'.

The figures for Southern India stood as follows, 37 percent educated, 21 percent having internet accessibility and 17 percent utilising the internet. In Central India, nearly 32 percent people were educated, 15 percent had internet accessibility while merely 12 percent used it. The figures for Eastern India are as follows, 26 percent educated, 9 percent had internet accessibility and 7 percent utilised internet. Figures for Western India translate into, 26 percent educated, 9 percent having internet accessibility and 7 percent utilising the internet (Table 9.2).

Table 9.1: Levels of Education and Digital Divide Across Regions in Rural India

Regions	Educated persons	Internet accessibility	Utilising internet
Northern India	39.3	21.5	19.3
Southern India	37.6	21.3	17.5
Central India	32.2	14.9	12.2
Eastern India	26.4	9.6	7.6
Western India	23.7	8.5	7.4
All-India	30.8	13.0	10.8

Note:
1. Figures represent percentage of persons.
2. For educated persons, the highest level has been taken as secondary level and above.

Source: Authors' calculation based on NSS 75th round data on 'Key Indicators of Household Social Consumption on Education in India'.

At the all-India level, both the level of education and internet usability was low as far as urban areas were concerned. The percentage of educated persons was merely 57 percent. More surprisingly, the internet accessibility was merely 37 percent, while only 33 percent used internet. In Northern India, nearly 61 percent of the people were found educated, 44 percent had internet accessibility while merely 41 percent used it.

The figure for Southern India stood at 58 percent being educated, 37 percent having internet accessibility and 33 percent utilising the internet. In Central India, nearly 61 percent of the people were educated, 40 percent had access to internet while merely 37 percent used it.

The figure for Eastern India stood at 56 percent being educated, 31 percent having access to internet and 28 percent utilising the same. Figures for Western India stood at 53 percent being educated, 30 percent having internet accessibility and 29 percent utilising the same (Figure 9.3).

Table 9.2: Levels of Education and Digital Divide Across Regions in Urban India

Regions	Educated persons	Internet accessibility	Utilising internet
Northern India	61.6	44.3	41.9
Southern India	57.9	37.7	33.1
Central India	61.4	40.6	36.9
Eastern India	55.9	31.44	28.1
Western India	53.5	30.45	28.9
All-India	57.5	37.1	33.8

Note:
1. Figures represent percentage of persons.
2. For educated persons, the highest level has been taken as secondary level and above.

Source: Authors' calculation based on NSS 75th round data on 'Key Indicators of Household Social Consumption on Education in India'.

Urban-rural gap in educational attainment was more in Western India (29.8 percent), followed by Eastern India (29.5 percent). It was the lowest in Southern India (20.3 percent). Rural-urban gap in utilising internet was more in Central India (24.7 percent), followed by Northern India (22.6 percent). It was the lowest in Southern India (15.6 percent).

Conclusion

Even though move towards computer literacy was introduced more than a couple of decades back, an enormous digital divide prevails in India, especially in the rural areas. In order to bridge this digital divide, we need to provide IT facilities at a reasonable price for commoners, accordingly train teachers, and provide schools and students with the right IT tools so that a solid digital user base can be created in the country.

Figure 9.3: Urban-Rural Gap in Education, Digital Divide Across Regions in India

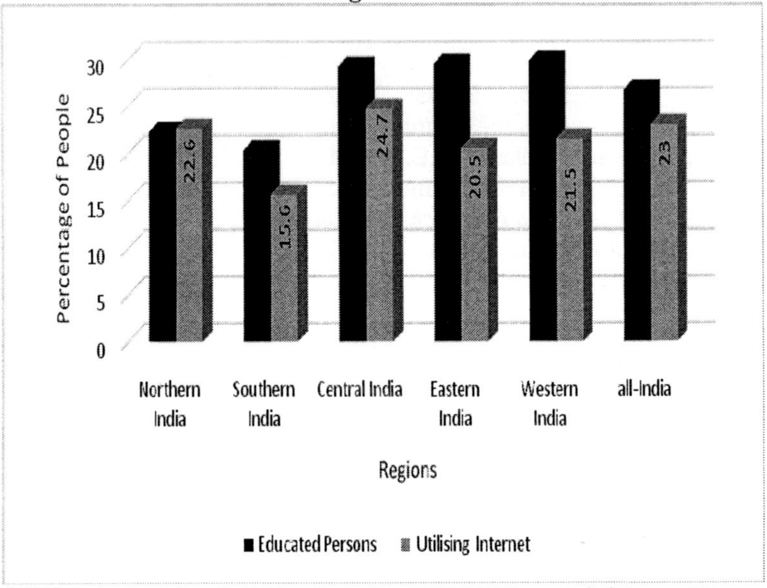

Source: Authors' calculation based on NSS 75th round data on 'Key Indicators of Household Social Consumption on Education in India'.

Endnotes

1. World Telecommunication Development Report (1998), Geneva: ITU (International Telecommunication Union), available at: http://www.itu.int/ITU-D/ict/publications/wtdr_02.
2. Tarman, B. (2003), "Digital Divide in Education", available at: https://www.researchgate.net/publication/215593349.
3. Thakur, G.K. (2014), "ICT and Digital Divide in Indian School System", *International Journal of Interdisciplinary and Multidisciplinary Studies*, 2(2), 34-38.
4. NSO report shows stark digital divide affects education, September

8, 2020), available at:
https://www.thehindu.com/news/national/nso-report-shows-stark-digital-divide-affects-education/article32554222.ece.

5. Bera, S.P. (2017), "Digital Divide in Brief", *IOSR Journal of Computer Engineering*, 19(4).
6. Bansode, S.Y. and Patil, S.K. (2011), "Bridging Digital Divide in India: Some Initiatives", *Asia Pacific Journal of Library and Information Science*, 1(1).
7. Singh, S. (2010), "Digital Divide in India: Measurement, Determinants and Policy for Addressing the Challenges in Bridging the Digital Divide", *International Journal of Innovation in the Digital Economy*, 20(2).
8. Panda, I., Chhatar, D.C. and Mharana, B. (2013), "A Brief View to Digital Divide in Indian Scenario", *International Journal of Scientific and Research Publications*, 3(12).
9. Kaur, K. and Singh, J. (2016), "ICT Diffusion and Digital Divide in India: Implications for Economic Policies", *Pacific Business Review International*, 1(2).
10. Mohanti, Pratap (2008), "Bridging Digital Divide: Role of ICT for Rural Development in India", IEEE, New Delhi.
11. Bridges (2001), "Spanning the Digital Divide", Bridges.org Report, available at:
http://www.bridges.org/spanningchpt4.html.
12. Chopra, H.S. (2006), "Digital Divide: An Indian Scenario", proceedings of the 2nd ICDL, December 5-8, New Delhi, pp. 232-239.
13. Cullen, R. (2001), "Addressing the Digital Divide", *Online Information Review*, 25, pp. 311-320.
14. Kumar, Rajendra (2005), "Bridging the Rural Digital Divide", *The Hindu*, April 12.
15. Government of India (2020), "Key Indicators of Household Social Consumption on Education in India", NSS 75th round.

10

Barriers of Digital Literacy for Financial Initiatives in Rural India

Elhamuddin Safi and Abdul Azeez N.P.

Introduction

Other than the agricultural-intensive economies and labour-intensive economies, the global economy is in transition to a *knowledge economy*, as an extension of an *information society* in information age led by innovations. The transition requires that the rules and practices that determined success in the industrial economy need rewriting in an interconnected, globalized economy where knowledge resources such as trade secrets and expertise are as critical as other economic resources.

Digital India is an initiative of the Government of India to integrate Government Ministries/Departments with the people of India. It aims at ensuring the availability of government services to citizens electronically by reducing paperwork. The initiative also includes plans to connect rural areas with high-speed internet networks. DI has three core components. These include creation of digital infrastructure, delivering services digitally and digital literacy.

A two-way platform will be created where both the service providers and the consumers stand to benefit. The public-private-partnership (PPP) model will be adopted selectively.

Digital India is a programme to transform India into a digitally empowered society and knowledge economy. It has the following components:

1. Digital India is a programme to prepare India for a knowledge future.

2. The focus is on being transformative—to realize IT + IT = IT.
3. The focus is on making technology central to enable change.

The Programme pulls together many existing schemes and these schemes will be restructured and re-focused. They will be implemented in a synchronized manner. Many elements are only process improvements with minimal cost.

The common branding of programmes as Digital India, highlights their transformative impact.

The vision of Digital India is centered on the following 3 key areas:

1. Digital infrastructure as a utility to every citizen.
2. Governance and services on demand.
3. Digital empowerment of citizens.

Under the Digital India mission, the government aims to target the following nine pillars:

1. Broadband highways.
2. Universal access to phones.
3. Public internet access programme.
4. E-governance–reforming government through technology.
5. E-kranti—electronic delivery of services.
6. Information for all.
7. Electronics manufacturing—target NET ZERO imports.
8. IT for jobs.
9. Early harvest programmes.

The hope for Digital India is not only dependent on the provision of internet facilities, but also largely depends on reduction in "digital divide", the gap between information-rich and information-poor people (Sharma, 2018, pp. 2-4), since 68.84 percent of the population (833.1 million people) lives in 6,40,867 villages across the country (Census, 2011).

Despite other knowledge, digital literacy and skill is a prerequisite for running up digital hubs; otherwise digitization would turn into a threat for all individuals (Helsper, 2011).

The importance of digital literacy and competency has

become the main agenda for policy makers and researchers to involve citizens in the digitized society (Iordache et al., 2017). It has been found that digital skills, competency and inclusion are paramount to ensure participation of individuals in the society (Van Deursen and Van Dijk, 2014). However, in a highly heterogenic society, it is not difficult to propagate and expand digital literacy? Yes, it may be but it does not mean that social-heterogeneity will not be converted to digital society. Iordache et al., (2017) unravelled the digital literacy concepts, skills, and competency by reviewing varied literature and found that a diversified society can be remedied by different digital literacy models.

Not only computers, but even the mobile technology has brought in new services, increased mobility, and has spearheaded unprecedented liberalization and competition (Marriott, 2006). According to Silva et al. (2019), digital finance is defined as, "the ability to use mobile devices by quickly authenticating identity, and making real-time payments". This paper aims to indicate various barriers towards digital literacy by assessing the digital literacy status in rural areas of India.

Objectives and Research Methodology

In this study, mixed research design has been used to systematically integrate qualitative and quantitative data. The term "mixed methods" refers to an emerging methodology of research that advances the systematic integration, or "mixing", of quantitative and qualitative data within a single investigation or sustained program of inquiry. Such kinds of methods provide a great potential to strengthen and enrich the analysis and findings of any evaluation (PCMH Research Methods Series, No. 13-0028-EF).

Literature Review

Even though digital literacy, digital skills, and digital competency have been used synonymously, there are conceptual differences between digital skills, digital literacy and digital competency. Ala-Mutka (2011, p. 18), defined competence as, “the ability to apply knowledge and skills in different contexts such as work, leisure, and learning”. Digital literacy refers to both competence and knowledge, while skills are assumed to be more technical features of these competence and knowledge (Van Deursen, 2010, p. 71).

According to the European Qualifications Framework (European Commission, 2008, p. 11), skill is an ability to apply knowledge while knowledge refers to “the body of facts, principles, theories and practices related to a field of work or study”. On the other hand, competence is a mixed term of knowledge and skill where both, knowledge and skill are applied for personal development. Van Deursen (2010) categorized skill as follows:

1. Operational skills.
2. Formal skills.
3. Information skills.
4. Strategic skills.

Digital literacy consists of a dynamic combination of mindset and behaviour that are employed to change and enhance skills through the use of digital information, technology, and media. Martin and Madigan (2006, p. 255), for example, outlined the concept of digital literacy and skills as follows, “digital literacy is awareness, attitude and ability of individuals to appropriately use digital tools and facilities to identify, access, manage, integrate, evaluate, analyse and synthesize digital resources, construct new knowledge centres, create media expressions, and communicate with others”.

Government of India Efforts for Financial Inclusion

According to National Strategy for Financial Inclusion, 2019-2024, India started its financial inclusion efforts way back in 1956 with the nationalization of life insurance companies and further nationalization of banks in 1969 and 1980, followed by the nationalization of insurance companies in 1972. Currently, the Reserve Bank of India (RBI) is a member of four working groups' viz. Standards, Implementation and Evaluation, Digital Financial Literacy, Financial Education for MSMEs and Core Competencies for Financial Literacy under the International Network for Financial Education (INFE), set up by the OECD.

Moreover, India began its National Strategy for Financial Inclusion (NSFI) in June 2017 under the supervision of Financial Inclusion Advisory Committee (FIAC). Under this strategy, the insights of various departments and stakeholders were taken into account, including the Department of Financial Services (DFS), Department of Economic Affairs (DEA), Ministry of Finance (MoF), RBI, SEBI, IRDAI, PFRDA, NABARD and NPCI.

National Strategy for Financial Inclusion, 2019-2024, targeted several sectors and regions for financial inclusion such as the MSMEs. MSMEs contribute nearly 31 percent to India's GDP, 45 percent to exports and provide employment opportunities to more than 11.1 crore skilled and semi-skilled people. As a meaty contributor to Indian economy, several programs have been launched for credit facilitation of this sector. These include, the National Mission for Capacity Building of Bankers for Financing MSME Sector' (NAMCABS), Certified Credit Counsellors (CCC) scheme, 'Udyami Mitra', Trade Receivables Discounting System (TReDS) platforms, and Pradhan Mantri Mudra Yojana (PMMY).

To spread financial inclusion, banks were instructed to open branches and provide ATMs facilities in rural areas. Despite the current development in expansion of financial inclusion and financial services, there are still perilous gaps remaining in the usage of financial services that require consideration of policy makers through necessary co-ordination and effective observing.

Based on the National Strategy for Financial Inclusion, 2019-2024, there are several challenges towards financial inclusion, as listed below:

1. Insufficient physical infrastructure and untrained staff,

especially in far flung areas of North-East region.

2. Internet and tele-connectivity in rural hinterland across the country is poor.
3. Certain value system and beliefs prevent women from having freedom and choice to access financial services.
4. Since competition is based on innovations, there is a strong need for market players to minimize risks in retail payment system from the financial stability perspective.

Government of India had set up the Financial Stability and Development Council (FSDC), which is mandated, *inter alia,* to focus on financial inclusion and financial literacy issues. In order to further strengthen the ongoing financial inclusion agenda in India, a high level Financial Inclusion Advisory Committee was constituted by the RBI. The Committee would pave the way for developing a viable and sustainable banking services delivery model focusing on accessible and affordable financial services, developing products and processes for rural and urban consumers presently outside the banking network and for suggesting appropriate regulatory framework to ensure that financial inclusion and financial stability move in tandem. India has, for a long time, recognized the social and economic imperatives for broader financial inclusion and has made an enormous contribution to economic development by finding innovative ways to empower the poor.

It is also considered that more than half of Indian people living in rural areas are isolated from the benefits of economic progress and digitalization. Even though India is the second fastest growing mobile market, it is still lagging in internet connectivity, deficiency in infrastructure and socio-cultural barriers, in recent times. To achieve the goal 'Digital India', and spread out digital finance and digitalization, it is important to give hands to poorer people in rural India as:

"Digital India is our dream for the nation. When I say 'Digital India'...it is not meant for the rich but for those who are poor". —Prime Minister Narendra Modi

Development of digital tools and the icon, picture and

symbol system in computer and mobile, make it easy for illiterate people to use them for multi-purpose activities, especially for digital finance and banking. Rajput and Nair (2013) stated that people who want to learn digital literacy can be educated or uneducated, irrespective of age, sex or status etc., but an educated person can easily learn and be familiar with digital technology. Government of India has been implementing several projects in this regard. NASSCOM Foundation has started the National Digital Literacy Mission (NDLM) with a vision to empower at least one person per household with crucial digital literacy skills by 2020.

Barriers to Digital Literacy

Based on National Digital Literacy Mission (NDLM) program, only one person per eligible household would be considered for training. In India, if 4.4 people per household are calculated and only one member of a household is trained, how would the remaining 3.4 members would be trained...is a big question.

In India, just 6.5 percent of the people are computer literate, 150 million households have an outreach to radio and television, more than 330 million households have access to mobile phones, and 31.2 percent of the population subscribes to internet via mobile phone. This gap indicates that there are millions of people who need to be educated for digital tools which call for a massive campaign for digital literacy. Even with the prevalent digital literacy gap between urban and rural India, there is a deepening male and female digital literacy gap also (Table 10.1).

Table 10.1: Digital Literacy Gap between Rural and Urban India

Ability	Rural		Urban	
	Male	Female	Male	Female
Able to operate a computer	12.6%	7%	37.5%	26.9%
Able to use internet	17.1%	8.5%	43.5%	30.1%

Source: Ministry of Statistics and Program Implementation, Government of India.

References

Ala-Mutka, K. (2011), "Mapping Digital Competence: Towards a Conceptual Understanding", European Commission Joint Research Centre, Institute for Prospective Technological Studies.

Bawden, D. (2008), "Origins and Concepts of Digital Literacy", in C. Lankshear (ed.), 'Digital Literacy: Concepts, Policies and Practices', New York, NY: Lang.

Chandramouli, C. and General, R. (2011), "Census of India, 2011: Provisional Population Totals", New Delhi: Government of India.

Gautam, N. K. and Gharu, Arya (2017), "Managing Digital Literacy in India", *International Journal of Engineering Technology Science and Research* (IJETSR), 4, 3.

Marriott, Michel, (2006), "Blacks Turn to Internet Highway, and Digital Divide Starts to Close", *The New York Times*, March 31.

Potter, W.J. (2004), "Theory of Media Literacy: A Cognitive Approach", Thousand Oaks, California: Sage Publications.

Purohit, Harsh, Niharika, Bharti and Anckur, Joshi (2009), "Partnering for Promotion of Digital Literacy among Women in Rajasthan through Bhartiya Model of Digital Literacy", Banasthali Vidyapeeth Working Paper Series: FMS/IT/002, available at:
http://ssrn.com/abstract=2665736.

Rajput, A. and Nair, K.K. (2013), "Significance of Digital Literacy in E-Governance", *The SIJ Transactions on Industrial, Financial and Business Management* (IFBM), 1(4), 136-141.

Sharma, Navneet Kumar (2018), "Challenges and Barriers to Bridging Digital Divide", *Library Waves*, 3, 2, 2455-2291.

Techataweewan, W. and Prasertsin, U. (2018), "Development of Digital Literacy Indicators for Thai Undergraduate Students Using Mixed Method Research", *Kasetsart Journal of Social Sciences*, 39(2), 215-221, available at:
https://doi.org/10.1016/j.kjss.2017.07.001.

11

Digital Financial Literacy: An Overview

V. Sonali

The main motive of digital literacy is to generate awareness amongst individuals about digitalization. Digital awareness is not only limited to the financial sector but also applicable in each and every sector so that the burden of paper work can be reduced. Financial literacy educates everyone how to manage their financial portfolio, provide useful data and familiarize people with various financial products.

Financial inclusion is nothing but an opportunity as to how one can invest their money or how funds can be utilized.

Financial Literacy and Digital Financial Literacy

Financial literacy is the possession of a set of skills and knowledge which allow an individual to make informed and effective decisions with all of his financial resources. Understanding basic financial concepts allows people to know how to navigate in the financial system.

India is a developing economy with focus on achieving sustainable development. To achieve sustainable development, it is important that all sections of the society get equal opportunity and participate in nation-building. Lack of awareness of digital financial literacy, especially among the rural population is a major challenge in the country, more so in light of the Government's recent demonetization and plans to make India a cashless economy. There is an urgent need to create awareness among the citizens, especially in rural and semi-urban areas regarding digital financial services and also enable/support in access to digital financial services options.

The best way to get more knowledge about digital finance

is to use various electronic means for doing financial transactions and making it a regular habit.

Importance of Financial Literacy

People with appropriate financial literacy training make better financial decisions and manage money better that those without such training. Financial literacy focuses on the ability to manage personal finance matters in an efficient manner, and it includes the knowledge of making appropriate decisions about personal finance such as investing, insurance, real estate, budgeting, retirement and tax planning. Financial literacy also involves the proficiency of financial principles and concepts such as financial planning, compound interest, managing debt, profitable savings techniques and the time value of money.

The main steps to achieving financial literacy include learning skills to create a budget, the ability to track spending, learning the techniques to pay off debt and effectively planning for retirement. These steps can also include counselling from a financial expert. Education about the topic involves understanding how money works, creating and achieving financial goals and managing internal and external financial challenges.

There are many advantages of financial literacy. Financial literacy helps individuals to become self-sufficient so that they can achieve financial stability. Those who understand the subject should be able to answer several questions about purchases, such as whether an item is required, whether it is affordable, and whether it an asset or a liability.

This skill can help a person develop a financial roadmap to identify what he earns, what he spends and what he owes. This topic also affects small business owners, who greatly contribute to economic growth and stability.

Lack of financial literacy can lead to owing large amounts of debt and making poor financial decisions. Similarly, financial illiteracy may lead to making poor financial choices that can have negative consequences on the financial well-being of an individual.

Financial illiteracy affects all ages and all socio-economic levels. Financial illiteracy causes many people to become victims of predatory lending, sub-prime mortgages, and fraud and high interest rates, potentially resulting in bad credit, bankruptcy or foreclosure.

Since the business environment is fiercely competitive, many businesses adopt malpractices and cut corners for growth and profitability. Poor customer services and malpractices such as mis-selling are often the result of such behaviour. Particularly in financial services, where the products are intangible and complex, customers can be duped easily. Hence, there is a need for careful decision-making on the part of a layman.

Products of Digital Finance

Online Banking: Nowadays, banks are offering digital services to meet every requirement of a customer with immediate response and high quality technical solutions, which are fast and easy. Below mentioned are few of the services that banks are providing to their customers without any charges.

1. Opening of accounts
2. Money transfer
3. Withdrawal
4. Deposits
5. Transfer money
6. Checking account balance
7. Mini statements
8. Loan management
9. Bill payments

Unified Payment System: This is the easiest and popular means of transferring and depositing money to anyone, anywhere. Earlier it was so pathetic to take out precious time and visit a bank and stand in a long queue to deposit or transfer money. However, thanks to the government initiatives in the domain of digital financial services, the UPI system was introduced, bringing alongside numerous solutions to banking problems apart from saving time. This procedure is completely safe, secured and a transaction can be done through any of the banks accounts. The only thing a customer needs to do is to install any of the UPI apps from Play Store and subsequently provide inputs regards their banking details viz. account number, account name, IFSC and registered mobile number for generating a secret and unique pin.

The following are some of apps available for UPI transactions:

- BHIM
- Paytm
- Cred
- PhonePe
- Google Tez
- Amazon Pay

Digital Wallet: This term can also be synonymously referred to as pocket wallet or mobile wallet. Earlier, an individual used to visit a bank or an ATM to withdraw cash. The most remarkable innovation on digital platform, post-demonetization, has been the digital wallet which can be used via smart phones, tablet or a smart watch. Various prominent digital wallets currently available are listed below:

1. Airtel Money
2. Mobikwik
3. Jio Money
4. Oxigen
5. Paytm
6. SBI Buddy
7. Freecharge
8. mRuppee
9. itzCash
10. Citrus Pay
11. Axis Bank Lime
12. ICICI Pockets

13. SpeedPay

Rewards, Coupons, Cashbacks: This is another way through which customers can be encouraged for digital money. This is only a strategy used by banks for customer engagement. This is a measure which is facilitated by apps for promoting digital money and making more transactions. For doing certain transactions, rewards, cash back, and coupons are extended to the users for better experience.

Target-specific Financial Literacy

One of the recommendations of the Committee on Medium-term Path on Financial Inclusion (Chairman: Deepak Mohanty) was *one-size-fits-all* approach for financial education which might be less than ideal as different target groups need different kinds of financial education. As a result, the content needs to be customised for different target groups.

The Financial Inclusion and Development Department of the Reserve Bank of India has come up with customised financial literacy content for five different target groups, namely farmers, small entrepreneurs, school children, self-help groups (SHGs), and senior citizens.

Entrepreneurs: Non-farm entrepreneurs can obtain credit facilities for both working capital and term loan requirements by getting a general credit card (GCC) from the bank. A GCC is issued as a smart card/debit card (biometric smart card compatible for use in the ATMs/handheld swipe machines and capable of storing adequate information of entrepreneur's identity, assets and credit profile, etc.). Wherever accounts are not digitized, the GCC may be issued as a card/passbook or a credit card-cum-passbook incorporating the name, address, photograph of the holder, particulars of borrowing limit, validity period, etc., for the time being which will serve as an identity card as well as facilitate recording of transactions on an ongoing basis. The limit on the card will be fixed by the bank on a case-to-case basis based on risk assessment. The rate of interest on the loans obtained through GCC will be decided by the bank. As an entrepreneur, one is expected to know how much the bank charges on his loan.

Farmers: Kisan Credit Card Scheme aims at providing timely and adequate credit to farmers to meet their needs at the time of crop production (cultivation expenses), besides meeting contingency expenses. It also covers expenses related to ancillary activities through simplified procedures in obtaining loans as and when needed.

Financial Literacy and Reserve Bank of India (RBI)

Financial inclusion and education are two important elements of RBI's developmental role in promoting financial literacy. Towards this end, RBI has created a critical volume of literature in 13 languages for banks and other stakeholders. The aim of this initiative is to create awareness about financial products and services, good financial practices, going digital and consumer protection.

The Financial Literacy Week is an initiative by RBI to promote awareness on key topics every year through a focused campaign. Financial Literacy Week, 2019 was observed from June 3 to 7, 2019 on the theme "farmers" and how they can benefit by being a part of the formal banking system. The messages disseminated during the week focused on responsible borrowing and agricultural finance.

The booklet 'Financial Awareness Messages (FAME)' provides basic financial literacy messages for the information of general public. It contains eleven financial awareness messages, such as documents to be submitted while opening a bank account (KYC), importance of budgeting, saving and responsible borrowing, maintaining a good credit score by repaying loans on time, banking at doorstep or in vicinity, knowing how to lodge complaints at the bank and with the banking ombudsman, use of electronic remittances, investing money only in registered entities etc.

RBI has developed tailored financial literacy contents for five target groups viz. farmers, small entrepreneurs, school children, self-help groups and senior citizens that can be used by the trainers in financial literacy programmes.

Audio visuals have been designed for the benefit of general public on topics relating to financial literacy. These audio visuals are on basic financial literacy, Unified Payments Interface (UPI) and going digital.

Earlier, the RBI had published a series of pictorial booklets. Under the 'Raju' title, it created literature pertaining to habit of savings and banking concepts. The 'Money Kumar' series simultaneously explained the role and functions of the RBI.

Ponzi Schemes and Scams

In this digital era, individuals have become prone to ponzi schemes and scams. Due care needs to be taken to avoid the following scenarios:

1. Promise of returns on investments that are much higher than those offered by the banks.
2. Schemes offering rewards for enrolling friends, family, and/ or appointing distributors.
3. Attractive marketing material with complex and new investment options, offering incentives for early registration.
4. Offer for free services from unknown entities and websites.
5. Entities offering financial products or services, not authorized by RBI, IRDAI, SEBI, and NHB.
6. Telephone calls which either offer rewards or threaten prosecution, penalty, etc.
7. Emails/SMS from unknown individuals or regulators or government organizations asking for your bank account details.

Conclusion

Digital finance has played a crucial role towards the economic growth of the country by providing a secured platform for everyone to execute safe transactions. To further the outreach of financial literacy amongst citizens, government needs to focus more on rural areas and among the old age groups, because this bracket is more or less unaware about digital finance. In spite of having bank accounts, people in this bracket still visit banks for every transaction, reposing lack of confidence in digital finance.

Economic theories have been formulated with the belief that human beings take rational decisions and always want to maximize or optimise benefits. However, most of the people do not take rational decisions when it comes to money and finance. Behavioural finance has created a huge body of evidence to support the idea that the so-called rational man is anything but rational. Many a time, our financial decisions are driven by greed, herd behaviour and emotions.

Financial literacy has assumed greater significance in the 21st century due to complex financial products, prevalence of fraudulent schemes, deregulation policies of regulators and government. Financial literacy enables one to manage one's personal finance in a prudent manner and achieve financial well-being. The objective of any financial literacy programme is to improve knowledge, skills and behaviour of individuals which will lead to awareness and action towards better management of their and family finances.

Appendix

Appendix

Payment and Settlement Systems in India: RBI's Vision Document, 2019-21

RBI's Vision Document on Payment and Settlement Systems, released on May 15, 2019, has the core theme of Empowering Exceptional (E) Payment Experience.

Payment and settlement systems are the backbone of any economy. Recent years have witnessed substantial developments in this area of activity across the country. The Reserve Bank of India (RBI), under powers from the Payment and Settlement Systems Act, 2007, has endeavoured to ensure that India has *state-of-the-art* payment and settlement systems that are not just safe and secure, but are also efficient, fast and affordable. Efforts in this direction have yielded handsome results. The planned development of the payment systems has been guided by RBI's Vision Documents for the payment and settlement systems in India which are being put out in the public domain since the year 2002, the last in this series was the Payment Systems Vision 2018. The current Vision Document outlines the road map for the three-year period spanning from 2019 to 2021.

Some of the positive outcomes of the developments during the period 2015-18 included the following:

1. Ushering introduction of new and innovative systems.
2. Distinctive shift from paper to electronic payment modes.
3. Sizeable increase in transaction turnover.
4. Customer-centric initiatives.
5. International recognition.

Growth in electronic payments has been substantial with retail payments reflecting large growth in volume terms, while the systemically important financial market infrastructures (SIFMIs), such as the real time gross settlement (RTGS) system and financial markets clearing through Clearing

Corporation of India Ltd. (CCIL), dominate in value terms.

New challenges have arisen requiring new strategies and planned efforts to address them. While building on the constructs and achievements of the previous Vision Documents, the Payment Systems Vision, 2021, recognises the need for continued emphasis on innovation, cyber security, financial inclusion, customer protection and competition.

1.1 Review of Achievements of the Vision 2018

The Payment Systems Vision, 2018, of the Reserve Bank envisaged building of 'best-in-class' payment and settlement systems for a *less-cash* India through the four strategic pillars of responsive regulation, robust infrastructure, effective supervision and customer centricity. The Vision 2018 has facilitated:

1. Continued decrease in the share of paper-based clearing instruments.
2. Consistent growth in individual segments of retail electronic payment systems such as the national electronic funds transfer (NEFT), immediate payments service (IMPS) and card transactions.
3. Increase in registered customer base for mobile banking.
4. Launch of new products like unified payments interface (UPI) and Bharat QR (BQR).
5. Significant growth in acceptance infrastructure.
6. Accelerated use of Aadhaar in payment systems.

An assessment of the achievements during the three years covered by Vision 2018 reveals that the goal posts indicated above have been accomplished. In respect of the accelerated use of Aadhaar in payment systems, the matter is under review in the light of the judgement of the Honourable Supreme Court regarding storage of Aadhaar data.

1.2 Payment Systems Vision, 2021

Vision Statement: Empower every Indian with access to a bouquet of e-payment options that is safe, secure, convenient, quick and affordable.

The Vision 2021 for payment and settlement systems in

India enhances the strong foundation built over the last two decades. While the pursuit towards a 'less cash' society continues, accompanied by the ambition to have a less-card India as well, the endeavour is to also ensure increased efficiency, uninterrupted availability of safe, secure, accessible and affordable payment systems as also to serve segments of the population which are hitherto untouched by the payment systems. The decade to follow will witness a revolutionary shift in the way Indian citizens use digital payment options and will also empower them with an e-payment experience that will be exceptionally safe, secure and truly world class.

Vision 2021 concentrates on a two-pronged approach of: (a) exceptional customer experience; and (b) enabling an eco-system which will result in this customer experience. With this in view, the Vision aims towards:

1. Enhancing the experience of customers.
2. Empowering payment system operators and service providers.
3. Enabling the eco-system and infrastructure.
4. Putting in place a forward-looking regulation.
5. Supported by a risk-focussed supervision.

To achieve the above, the Vision envisages four goal-posts (4Cs): competition, cost, convenience and confidence.

For enhancement of **competition** in the payment systems landscape, specific thrust areas like creating regulatory sandbox, authorising new players etc. have been incorporated. This along with the presence of multiple players in the market is expected to achieve optimal **cost** for the customers. Freer access with availability of multiple payment system options anytime-anywhere should cater to the requirement of **convenience**. The 'no-compromise' approach towards safety of payment systems should address security vulnerabilities to retain customer **confidence**.

It is recognised that cash entails a significant cost to the whole economic system, including consumers. Migration to digital modes of making a payment can obviate some of these costs and can give customers a friction-free and enjoyable experience. Giving them multiple options is expected to make this experience exceptional, apart from furthering growth measurable in terms of digital payments turnover to GDP.

The savings achieved at all levels on account of digitisation of payments need to be considered in pricing of these services to the end customers. Payment system operators (PSOs) need to consider cost of accessing and managing transactions and accordingly price their services. The aim is towards progressive reduction in 'per-transaction' cost to customers keeping in view the marginal cost advantage with increase in the number of transactions. The need to move towards marginal cost of pricing based on volume of transactions handled needs no over-emphasis.

1.3 Expected Outcomes of Vision 2021

The Payment Systems Vision, 2021, covers the period up to December 2021.

Vision 2021 focuses on further enhancements and improvements in all facets of payment systems.

With concerted efforts and involvement of all stakeholders, the four goal-posts of Vision 2021 with 36 specific action points over the 36-month timeframe will have the following 12 specific outcomes:

1. Further decrease in the share of paper-based clearing as a percentage of retail payments, particularly in terms of number of paper instruments processed. Given the current trend in cheque usage and the thrust to shift to digitised transactions it is expected that the volume of cheque-based payments would be less than 2.0 percent of the retail electronic transactions by 2021.
2. Accelerated growth in individual retail electronic payment systems, both in terms of number of transactions and increased availability. Payment systems like UPI/IMPS are likely to register average annualised growth of over 100 percent and NEFT at 40 percent over the Vision period.

The number of digital transactions is expected to increase more than four times from 2,069 crore in December 2018 to 8,707 crore by December 2021.

3. Measurably, the digital payment transaction turnover vis-à-vis GDP (at market prices-current price) is expected to further increase to 10.37 in 2019, 12.29 in 2020 and 14.80 in 2021. Payment transaction turnover, including CCIL transactions and paper, is expected to be 22.30 times the GDP (at market prices-current price) by December 2021.
4. Increase in use of digital modes of payment for purchase of goods and services through increase in debit card transactions at PoS (35 percent increase during the Vision period) and continued growth in PPI transactions.
5. Usage of debit cards at PoS transactions is expected to be at least 44 percent of total debit card transactions (at PoS + ATM). In value terms it is 15.2 percent in 2018-19 (5.2 percent in 2014-15) which is expected to be 22 percent by end-2021.
6. Increased deployment of card acceptance infrastructure across the country including at smaller centres with a substantial portion of the infrastructure taking care of processing contactless card payments. Given the current growth trend it is expected to have 5 mn active PoS by end-2021; digital PoS (QR code) is also expected to increase substantially; and the total card acceptance infrastructure will be upscaled to six times present levels by end-2021. This is expected to support aim of cash-lite economy and also shift cash on delivery (CoD) transactions to digital modes for e-commerce.
7. While no specific target is considered for cash in circulation, the enhanced availability of PoS infrastructure is expected to reduce demand for cash and thus overtime, achieve reduction in cash in circulation (CIC) as a percentage of GDP.
8. Further facilitation of mobile based payment transactions as gauged on basis of the registered customer base

(expected increase of 50 percent considering the base effect).

9. Enhanced usage of electronic payment systems is expected to reduce the marginal cost given the additional volume. The pricing of such services to customers should, over the vision period, show reduction of at least a 100 bps from current levels. Plus, a shift from ad valorem rates to per transaction rates is envisaged, as usage of a system is irrespective of the value of a transaction.
10. Security of systems and customer centricity as reflected by

- Decrease in Technical Declines reported across various payment systems by 10 percent year-on-year.
- Reduction in Business Declines reported across various payment systems by 5 percent year-on-year. This will be achieved through targeted hand-holding of merchants and customers with customised campaigns by partnering with system operators and system participants.
- Improvement in turn around time (TAT) for resolution of customer complaints by PSOs.

11. FTS [fraud to sales (fraud value/sales value) x 10,000] count for payment systems is expected to be less than 10 bps for most of the payment systems.
12. Enhanced healthy competition in the payments space and establishment of new PSOs during the Vision period is envisaged.

1.4 Specific Initiatives

1.4.1 Customers:

A. Affordable, Accessible and Inclusive Services: The Indian payment ecosystem and its constituents are likely to respond well when processes are affordable, and accessibility is simple and wide spread. While the approach of the Reserve Bank will continue to be of minimal intervention in the pricing of charges to customers for digital payments, all efforts will be made towards facilitating the operation of payment systems which are efficient and price-attractive. To this end, service providers should set up pricing structures that are transparent, affordable and do not restrict public from accessing payment system services. The basis shall have to be that pricing is reasonable to encourage usage and also pass-on to the customer the benefit of cost saved on managing cash in the system. The Reserve Bank will require service providers to bring about transparency in pricing. Reserve Bank would consider a review of its instructions on customer charge for its payment systems and shift from transaction value-based pricing slabs to a fixed minimum transaction-based pricing. The approach to pricing should be towards recovery of marginal costs and to migrate to a low margin-high volume regime.

B. Harmonising Turnaround Time for Resolution of Customer Complaints, Including for Card Transactions: There is need for harmonising the TAT of customer complaints and requisite chargebacks. Such time lines should be reasonable and also in alignment with the instructions issued in respect of customer liability for unauthorised electronic payment transactions. The Reserve Bank will be addressing the various facets in this regard, with the objective of optimal time lines expected to result in customer delight and certainty of conclusion. Recourse to technology-driven dispute redressal mechanisms that are rule-based, transparent, customer-friendly and involve minimum (or no) manual intervention will be advocated/encouraged/appreciated.

C. Setting Up A 24x7 Helpline: Customer experience can be enhanced with a general centralised helpline for addressing customer queries in respect of various digital payment products, security aspects, recourse mechanism, etc. This will not only build trust and confidence but also reduce expenditure (both financial and human resources) otherwise incurred on addressing complaints and grievances. The payment service industry level self-regulatory organisation (SRO) proposed in this Vision can facilitate the setting up of an industry wide 24x7 helpline and the large-scale use of technology for customer assistance and complaint redressal.

D. Creating Awareness: To give thrust to the regulatory interventions on customer awareness, an industry level initiative needs to be taken for building awareness through generic advertisements and systematically planned customer orientation programmes. Equally important is to create customer awareness for basic cyber-security hygiene. Bankers and operators of the payments systems would have to ensure awareness at their end for strictly following defined secure operational processes. Creation of a universal icon/symbol set for basic use cases/operations in the area of retail electronic payments will also be explored during the period of this Vision document. Ensuring involvement of and co-operation from all stakeholders can help in achieving a very secure and convenient payment environment, with attendant reduction of business declines, and maybe, technical declines as well.

E. Conducting Customer Awareness Surveys: Customer surveys to gauge awareness and usage of various payment services, including digital payment systems amongst various stakeholders and individuals would be undertaken by the Reserve Bank. The findings of such surveys will be an important component for policy formulation. Repeated surveys in a location will help assess efficacy impact of various targeted interventions.

F. Internal Ombudsman by Payment System Operators (PSOs): The terms and conditions for authorisation of various payment systems by the Reserve Bank require them to put in place a grievance redressal mechanism. The Reserve Bank has also put in place an ombudsman scheme for digital transactions. While PSOs have set up their own mechanism for addressing customer complaints, there is a need to formalise an internal ombudsman in the PSOs so that there is an avenue for swift and cost-effective complaint redressal mechanism within the organisation.

G. Review of Corridors and Charges for Inbound Cross Border Remittances: Remittances play a crucial role for developing economies and have significant welfare implications. While the quantum of remittances depends on a number of factors, the cost of remitting funds is increasingly becoming a key element influencing the size of remittances. High cost of remittance made through formal channels may drive customers to informal channels which are less secure and prone to misuse. The G20 has prioritised the issue of cost of remittances in its agenda and is encouraging appropriate policies at the country level. India has already taken several measures to liberalise remittance schemes to drive competition and thereby reduce costs. Some of the initiatives include facilitating the appointment of more intermediaries/money transfer agents, introducing more official channels to route cross-border remittances, receipt of foreign inward remittances directly into the bank accounts of beneficiaries under the Money Transfer Service Scheme (MTSS), etc.

In order to infuse fair competition in this sphere and bring in transparency in costs, RBI will examine the role that payment services providers (PSPs) can play to ensure friction free remittances at lower cost.

1.4.2 System Operators and Service Providers:

A. Self-Regulatory Organisation (SRO): Industry self-governance is an important feature in modern economies which is also useful for industry wide smooth operations and development. With time, bodies representing interests of certain segments of PSOs have evolved and have been engaging with the regulator. There is a need for self-regulatory governance framework to foster best practices on important aspects like security, customer protection, pricing, etc. Such an organisation can be constituted to cover the entire gamut of digital PSOs, including retail products of National Payments Corporation of India (NPCI). The SRO will serve as a two-way communication channel between the players and the regulator/supervisor. The SRO will of course work towards establishing minimum benchmarks, standards and help discipline rogue behaviour.

B. Creating an Environment to Encourage and Facilitate Innovation through Collaborative Competition: As announced in the second bi-monthly monetary policy statement 2018-19, that the Reserve Bank would be publishing a consultation paper on the policy to encourage more players to participate in and promote pan-India payment platforms, to give a fillip to innovation and competition. The framework finalised after such consultations and discussions would be implemented. To encourage competition in existing payment systems, a review would be undertaken to consider authorisation of new players including one/few pan-India umbrella organisation/s.

A framework, transparently delineating minimum entry requirements for any PSO, would also be made public. Need for existing authorised PSOs to essentially have physical presence in India for operating payment systems would also be explored. Increased use of technology in all spheres of the payment system ecospace will be actively encouraged and appreciated. A review of existing policy would be undertaken to encourage/facilitate healthy competition and level playing field among banks and non-banks.

C. Feature Phone-based Payment Services: Availability of mobile telephony devices has democratised payments. As on February 28, 2019, there were 1,184 million wireless telephone subscribers and 532 million wireless broad band subscribers [as per data from Telecom Regulatory Authority of India (TRAI)]. While various reports indicate more than 350 million smartphone users in the country, a large user base of feature phones exists. General innovation in mobile payment services has focussed or supported app-based access limited to smartphones and such devices. There is a need to innovate payment services for feature phones to provide the necessary thrust towards enhanced adoption of digital payments by various strata of society which will be vigorously followed for implementation.

D. Off-Line Payment Solutions: Consumer behaviour has

been driving growth of digital payment systems as more and more consumers are embracing mobile technology. Though mobile internet speed has risen, connectivity issues remain unresolved in large areas. Therefore, providing an option of off-line payments through mobile devices for furthering the adoption of digital payments shall be a focus area during this Vision period.

E. USSD Based Payment Services: The available USSD based services require additional push through review of customer cost and enhanced usage through participation. The payment service providers may add features to scale up the security of the transactions, irrespective of the device security level/environment.

F. National Settlement Services: Banks are required to have different settlement accounts for settling card transactions with different card networks. To bring in more efficiency in the system and making the process more graceful, the Reserve Bank shall examine the feasibility of having a single national settlement account for all authorised card networks in consultation with the stakeholders.

1.4.3 Eco-System and Infrastructure:

A. Availability of Retail Payment Systems: Ease of use is often the reason for choosing one platform over the other by the customers looking for instantaneous transactions with confirmation. Reserve Bank would examine the need to consider uninterrupted and round-the-clock availability of various payment systems; gradual enhancement of limits, including differential day-night, holiday limits for transactions, subject to risk management and liquidity management; etc. The need for extending availability of NEFT on a 24x7 basis to facilitate beyond the banking hour fund transfer needs would be examined. Need to add more features to NEFT (faster settlements, staggered payments) will also be examined. Reserve Bank of India will also examine the possibility to extend the timings for customer transactions in RTGS, based on industry preparedness and customer demand.

B. Global Outreach of Payment Systems: India is home to several innovative digital payment products which are available to the public at low cost anytime anywhere. Many countries have expressed interest in partnering in this growth and replicating our products based on their country specific requirements. Specific interests/requests are being received for implementing CTS, NEFT, UPI, messaging solutions, etc., by certain jurisdictions. There is scope for enhancing global outreach of our payment systems, including remittance services, through active participation and co-operation in international and regional fora by collaborating and contributing to standard setting. RBI will continue to actively participate, involve and engage in discussions in international standard-setting bodies. Leadership role towards regional co-operation in payment systems is also envisaged.

C. Widen Scope, Use and Reach of Domestic Cards: Domestic cards have stabilised well and the potential for their large-scale use is high. Efforts will be made to increase the scope, coverage and usage of domestic cards, including the RuPay card scheme which was launched in March 2012. Collaborative effort will be initiated among NPCI, banks and the Government to widen and deepen the scope/usage of RuPay cards to enhance its brand value internationally.

D. Building Capability to Process Transactions of One System in another System: Interoperability of payment systems will be a watch word during the ensuing three-year period. Various retail payment systems will be encouraged to have this feature which provides benefits to all stake holders. The role of standardisation and the use of universally accepted standards will also be enhanced. Inter-operability in and among payment system operators/players will be vigorously pursued.

E. Acceptance Infrastructure: Address Supply Side Issues: Acceptance infrastructure, particularly point-of-sale (PoS) terminals/mobile PoS/asset-light terminals, as a percentage of the total number of debit/credit cards is low.

There is a need to increase the penetration of acceptance infrastructure in the country. The infrastructure will be upscaled to at least six times of the present levels in the next three years' time.

- **Acquirers:** Explore the option of permitting acquiring PoS infrastructure by all regulated entities, subject to regulatory clearance/no objection certificates. Increase in acquirers, like regional rural banks and non-banking financial companies, to cover a large section of establishments.
- **Innovation-based New Devices:** Innovation towards low-cost acceptance devices will be encouraged with a view towards cost reduction, enhanced safety and ubiquitousness.
- **Acceptance Development Fund (ADF):** Creation of an ADF to subsidise acquirers for deploying PoS acceptance infrastructure in tier-3 to tier-6 centres. This would help in facilitating innovation and reducing cost of such transactions.
- **Bharat QR (BQR):** Enhanced usage of signed and encrypted BQR as proactive preventive measure for secure payments.

F. Increased Coverage of the Cheque Truncation System (CTS): Since cheques continue to be an important payment instrument, steps would be taken to enhance the security and efficiency of the present CTS mechanism, including bringing in uniformity and harmony in processes across the three cheque processing grids, apart from steps towards increased coverage and a single settlement. Coverage will be increased across more locations including examining improvement in processes/features and discontinuing recourse to Paper to Follow (P2F) across all State Governments.

G. Trade Receivables Discounting System (TReDS): MSMEs face constraints in obtaining adequate finance given their inability to readily convert their trade receivables into liquid funds. TReDS was envisaged for resolving the liquidity crunch faced by MSMEs by facilitating the financing of their trade receivables from corporate and other buyers, including Government Departments and public sector undertakings (PSUs), through multiple financiers. As on date, three TReDS platforms are operational. The ecosystem is at a nascent stage; thus, over the Vision period, guidelines would be reviewed to provide maximum traction to the platform for achieving the goals of MSME financing by enabling re-discounting, considering some participation of non-MSMEs, expanding financier categories, increasing the number of platforms, on boarding more buyers, etc.

H. Geo-Tagging of Payment System Touch Points: In order to measure the adoption of digital payments, it is essential to have geographical location of the payment system touch points [bank branches, ATMs, PoS terminals, Business Correspondents (BCs), etc.] across the country. The Reserve Bank is examining a framework to capture the location and business details of commercial bank branches, ATMs and BCs. It is envisaged to extend a similar framework to capture and maintain information about PoS terminals and other payment system touch points as well.

1.4.4 Regulation:

A. Fostering Innovation in a Responsible Environment through Regulatory Sandbox: The regulatory sandbox approach has been gaining traction in several jurisdictions. A sandbox approach to regulation would help enable innovation in digital payments while avoiding any systemic risks. The Reserve Bank's Working Group Report on FinTech and Digital Banking recommended developing a framework for regulatory sandboxes. Given the evolving nature of payment instruments and technologies used to provide payment services, a framework for a regulatory sandbox for payment systems would be designed to provide a controlled environment, with certain regulatory exemptions, to allow experimentation of new payment system products by traditional and non-traditional players.

B. System Capacity and Scalability: The current approach to authorisation for payment systems is liberal with no prescriptions and/or assessment responsibilities on the payment service providers in terms of performance metrics like uptime, technical declines, capacity, etc. for systems operated by them. At the infant stage of development, this measure was considered necessary to enable service providers to build and enhance capabilities over time. As payment systems have since come a long way, and there is an increasing expectation that the systems should be robust and resilient, a framework for an ongoing assessment of the performance of retail payment systems would be designed. Need for prescribing explicit exit criteria of payment systems and payment system operators based on a transparent point-of-arrival metrics will also be explored.

C. Contactless Payments and Tokenisation: Contactless payments, while decreasing the time taken for payment checkout, also ease payments for small ticket payment transactions. Tokenisation technologies often form the basis of facilitating seamless e-commerce experiences fuelled by mobile and other connected devices. The rapid growth in devices provides a significant opportunity for payments through any form factor and anywhere. For digital payments to take advantage of this opportunity, an appropriate regulatory framework built on the principles of innovation, transparency and consumer control is required. Reserve Bank has already recognized this and authorised certain players to offer mobile payment solutions driven by secure tokenisation standards. RBI would consider a broad-based framework for other payment experiences, keeping in mind customer liability issues and security of authentication mechanisms.

D. Review of Membership of Centralised Payment Systems: The Reserve Bank continuously receives requests and feedback for payment infrastructure access neutrality between banks and non-banks. RBI has already permitted participation of non-banks in certain payment infrastructure;

RBI will initiate discussion to develop a framework for settlement risk management with increased participation of non-banks.

E. Increasing Lei Usage for Large Value Cross Border Payments: Legal Entity Identifier (LEI) system envisages identification of unique parties to financial transactions across the globe and is designed as an important component for improvement in financial data across the globe. Cross border retail payments are generally less transparent and more expensive than domestic transactions. Given the nature of cross border transactions, there is a case for exploring the option of using LEI to identify the payment service providers, their agents and distributors, in respect of cross border services, particularly for large value payments, including expanding the implementation across all the identified segments.

F. Encourage Adoption of New Technologies Including DLT for Enhancement of Digital Payment Services: Technology has been at the centre of payment systems innovation and development. Adoption of distributed ledger technology (DLT) for financial services has been a subject of interest. Various views espouse that adoption of DLT can enhance the operations of payment systems by improving the quality of data and providing additional information for payment transaction, which help automated reconciliation and reversal with high degree of precision. Adoption of DLT will be considered to facilitate industry wide adoption for areas which can benefit from this technology.

G. E-Mandates/Standing Instructions: The Reserve Bank has been receiving requests for allowing e-mandate/standing instructions-based automation of periodically recurring, non-discretionary payments. The Reserve Bank will consider implementation of e-mandates/standing instructions for retail payment systems, subject to customer protection and adequate safeguards like authenticating payment instrument registration, mandating transaction limits, segments, etc.

H. Security Aspects of Mobile Payments: The guidelines for mobile banking issued by the Reserve Bank indicate the technological and security standards which the banks may comply with while providing mobile banking services to their customers. The Reserve Bank would issue specific standards which the banks providing mobile payment services shall comply with, mandate minimum requirements, highlight best practices and initiate discussion on risks emerging from innovative payment channels through emerging technologies including artificial intelligence, internet of things devices, wearables, etc.

I. Regulation of Payment Gateway Service Providers and Payment Aggregators: The growth of online payment transactions has led to increasing role of payment gateway service providers. The current guidelines on payment gateway operations (monitored through banks) are indirect and address only a few specific aspects of their functioning. The Reserve Bank has initiated discussion on examining the need for separate guidelines for payments related activities of these entities which will be taken forward during the Vision period.

J. Inter-Regulatory and Intra-Regulatory Co-Ordination: In order to have a co-ordinated approach towards regulation, the Reserve Bank shall engage with the other sectoral regulators—SEBI, IRDA, TRAI, etc., to remove frictions in regulation and ease system operator/customer comfort. The endeavour will also to have a co-ordinated approach to regulation and supervision within Reserve Bank across the different related departments—Department of Banking Regulation, Department of Banking Supervision, Department of Non-Banking Regulation, Department of Co-operative Banking Regulation, Financial Markets Regulation Department, Financial Markets Operations Department, Foreign Exchange Department, Customer Education and Protection Department, Department of Information Technology, Department of Economic and Policy Research, Department of Statistics and Information Management, Department of Government and Bank Accounts, etc. Similar engagements with the subsidiaries of Reserve Bank—Institute for Development and Research in Banking Technology (IDRBT), Reserve Bank Information Technology Pvt. Ltd. (ReBIT), etc., will be pursued.

1.4.5 Risk-Focussed Supervision

A. Proportionate Oversight for Maintaining Integrity of Payment Systems: Security is pivotal and risk management practices should be implemented with conservativeness in approach and ruthlessness in implementation across each and every product. Cyber risks are increasing rampantly with advancement in technology and increasing adoption of digital services, whether financial or otherwise, are bringing these issues to the forefront. This issue becomes grave given the fact that the nature of threat is dynamic and keeps changing rapidly. The interconnected systems are as safe as their weakest link. There is, therefore, a need for both security against possible cyber-attacks and resilience in the eventuality of such attacks. All payment systems should display explicit levels of safety. It would be necessary that systems not only meet the requirements of safety but are also subjected to safety audits at periodic intervals.

The Reserve Bank undertakes oversight of the payment systems through onsite supervision and off-site surveillance. There is a prescription of self-assessment by the PSOs, which are also required to subject their systems to IS audit through CERT empanelled auditors. For transparency and clarity, there is a need for disclosed supervisory framework for all the stake holders to better understand their roles and responsibilities. The need for publishing oversight reports in public domain by the Reserve Bank would be considered. The feasibility of oversight of cross border entities with the help of information sharing MoUs with overseas regulators will also be examined. The oversight framework for PSOs would also include data reporting and analytics requirements for PSOs.

The existing penalty framework for payment system operators will be reviewed and modified, if required, to make the process more transparent and achieve the expected outcomes.

In consultation with the CSITE Cell of the Reserve Bank, the need to subject payment system operators to the same rigour for cyber security preparedness as the other entities in the financial sector will be looked into.

B. Third Party Risk Management and System-Wide Security: The Reserve Bank had earlier issued guidelines on managing risks in respect of outsourcing of financial services by banks. The need for a separate regulatory framework for outsourcing arrangements by non-bank payment service providers would be examined given the current trend of outsourcing arrangements and the need for security control and clarity of roles and responsibilities of the regulated entities. Such a framework would consider the risks associated with data access, confidentiality, integrity, sovereignty, recoverability, regulatory compliance and auditing. Such a framework would also consider overall security of the digital payments ecosystem by covering the entire payment transaction chain, including the need for establishing end point security. Adoption of PCI (Payment Card Industry) standards can be considered as a desirable best practice by all the entities in a payment transaction chain, irrespective of their status as a regulated entity or otherwise. Need to customise PCI standards to better suit/reflect Indian situations will also be explored.

C. Framework for Collecting Data on Frauds in Payment Systems: To further strengthen the confidence in the payment systems and minimise instances of frauds, there is a need to monitor the types of frauds that may be taking place in various payment systems. To this end, there is a need to share fraud related data for payment systems. Such data can be used analytically for differentiating fraudulent and legitimate transactions; oversight and supervision, and also for providing guidelines to entities for minimising risks of similar frauds. This would also help in improving resilience and trust in the system. The Reserve Bank would promote use of such analytics to proactively identify instances and aspire for prediction of frauds to help instant response and recovery actions, such as blocking irregular transactions, before the payment authorisation. The fraud data will be used to influence regulatory decisions and for reducing the incidence and level of frauds in the payments ecospace.

D. Drafting a Framework for Testing Resilience of Payment Systems: With the introduction of alternate modes of electronic payments, both for the financial markets, and for businesses and individuals, the resilience of the payment systems has gained importance. Here, resilience refers to the ability to continue to operate even if a system has failed completely by switching activity to a separate system or process or a combination of both. A framework would be drafted for the same. The framework shall also include business continuity and infrastructure redundancy preparedness.

E. Benchmarking India's Payment Systems: An efficient payment system reduces the cost of exchanging goods and services and is indispensable to the functioning of the intra-bank, inter-bank, money and capital markets. The past decade has been witnessing a number of innovations, especially in retail payments. The Reserve Bank shall conduct an exercise which will aim at benchmarking India's payment systems and gauge India's standing against major countries across all payment systems and payment instruments. Efforts will be towards improving the performance and standing of our payment systems vis-à-vis international/cross-country best practices. The learning points will also be used to improve existing payment system features in the interest of reducing frictions and enhancing acceptance and usage levels. The endeavour shall also be to repeat the benchmarking exercise by expanding coverage and features.

Index

Index